Praise for
The Zen Executive

The Zen Executive is a book whose time has come. It aptly and beautifully demonstrates how integrating spiritual principles with executive leadership principles is not only possible but is critical to the fundamental health and wealth of any organization and the individuals within it. Jim Blake has written a deeply insightful, practical, and compelling guide for not only those in the executive suite, but for anyone desiring to live, work, and lead in a more thoughtful, kind, and heart-centered way, grounded in love, and with compassion as their bottom line. This is the kind of inspired leadership we need for these times.

Michael Bernard Beckwith

Founder and CEO, Agape International Spiritual Center

Author of *Life Visioning* and *Spiritual Liberation*

Spirituality in leadership? Most of us have a level of spirituality that guides us through our days, but even at work? That is the perfect place to be a kinder, more thoughtful person. Jim Blake shares his vast experience as a seeker and leader in ***The Zen Executive***. Written with understanding, humor, and genuine caring, this is a book to help entrepreneurs, teams, and anyone to live with authenticity in all areas of their world.

Sharon Salzberg

Author of *Real Happiness at Work*
and *Real Change*

Jim Blake offers a practical and whole-systems guide that all leaders need to flourish from the inside out. ***The Zen Executive*** is a pragmatic and compassionate inquiry into the inner workings that cultivate deep transformative shifts in self, community, and society.

Ina Gjikondi

Director, Executive Education and Coaching
The George Washington University
Center for Excellence in Public Leadership

It takes courage to dare to be a different kind of leader, one who blends compassion and well-being of others with performance and profit. Jim Blake provides the steps for those who are willing to not only lead but to change lives professionally and personally—which benefits all. ***The Zen Executive*** provides valuable information for any leader seeking an authentic and fulfilling life and career.

Scott Shute

Author of *The Full Body Yes*

Former head of Mindfulness and Compassion Programs at LinkedIn

Leaders who are integrating compassion, intuition, and self-care practices into mission-driven leadership will find Jim Blake's ***The Zen Executive*** of great value.

Ken Druck, Ph.D.

Author of *The Real Rules of Life*

Speaker and organizational consultant

THE ZEN EXECUTIVE

THE ZEN EXECUTIVE

Gems of Wisdom for Enlightened Leadership

JIM BLAKE

unity Books

Unity Village, MO 64065-0001

The Zen Executive

 For information, address Unity Books, 1901 NW Blue Parkway, Unity Village, MO 64065-0001.

Unity Books are available at special discounts for bulk purchases for study groups, book clubs, sales promotions, book signings, or fundraising. To place an order, call the Unity Customer Care Department at 816-251-3571 or email *wholesaleaccts@unityonline.org*.

Cover design: Charles McStravick

Interior design: Hailee Pavey

ISBN: 978-0-87159-417-4

Library of Congress Control Number: 2021952543

Canada BN: 13252 0933 RT

Dedication

I dedicate this book to Denise Blake, my best friend, life partner, and love of my life. More times than I can count, she saw the potential in me that I was unable to see in myself. Any success I have been blessed with has been a result of her unwavering belief in me and support of me as I have pursued my dreams.

Foreword

Jim Blake is not the author you would expect. His résumé, his life experiences, and his compelling physical presence don't usually coexist in one person so coherently. As you read *The Zen Executive*, you will find the wisdom he shares is humble, practical, and useful in any setting. In my journey with Jim the past 12 years, I have watched him grow into a powerful business and spiritual leader. The breadth of his business experience combined with his spiritual wisdom makes this a perfect book for everyone to own and use, not only for leadership but everyday relationships.

More eloquently than I can express here, Jim straightforwardly addresses some of the biggest challenges facing businesses today, in both for-profit and not-for-profit companies. Both rely on the same essential resources: money, talent, innovation, and rejuvenation. Jim draws from lessons learned in his corporate career as well as his leadership of a 130-year-old spiritual institution to illustrate in *The Zen Executive* how to improve the culture of any organization. What matters most in successful leadership is taking the time to be with, listen to, and foster your team's well-being. As Jim points out, those are spiritual practices; they also happen to be highly effective in business and are exactly what makes a Zen executive.

I met Jim Blake when I was a student in the Unity Institute® and Seminary Master of Divinity program. Previously, I worked for decades in the New York for-profit theater world, working my way up from a company member to a director/choreographer, in charge of multimillion-dollar productions at the same time I was running my floral event company serving high-end corporate and private clients. I learned about thriving through adversity, putting together winning teams, developing diverse streams of income, and delivering exceptional products. But my journey with Jim would take me to new levels of understanding about the challenges and opportunities when making business decisions about money, people, and property.

When I started in seminary, Jim was working for Unity World Headquarters as vice president of IT. He was an imposing physical figure—more than 6 feet tall with a linebacker's build and a shaved head—not what I expected from a computer techie. I was living with several other students in 1950s-era housing on campus, and our concrete building had no access to Wi-Fi. Jim listened to us and created a simple solution, taking the time to help this small group of students—essentially guests on campus—even though he was in charge of the computer and digital needs for more than 300 employees in the Unity organization. Little did I know his thoughtfulness and willingness to serve would be the hallmark of my relationship with Jim.

Years later, after Jim had left Unity for the corporate world then returned as CEO, I was asked to serve on the Board of Directors. In my interview with Jim and the entire board, he mentioned that one of his strategic goals was outreach to the LGBTQIA+ community. Because of the trauma many gay people have experienced through religion, I suggested the only way to make that work would be to have LGBTQIA+ leaders in visible positions. He paused, smiled, then gently replied, "That's why I asked you if you would be interested in joining the board." In *The Zen Executive*, Jim shows us that what we do is much more important than what we say.

Today, as the board chair for Unity World Headquarters, I connect with Jim weekly as we navigate, steward, and evolve our cherished institution. I witness how he masterfully navigates leading a spiritual organization while serving a diverse and not necessarily spiritual or religious workforce. He also has a knack for asking perceptive questions—sometimes uncomfortable questions—and reveals in this book how to question why we do what we do as business leaders, what our work means to us, and when to change course.

Jim is the right person at the right time for our organization, and his book is the right tool now for all of us who are leading teams, companies, and communities. Whether you are a business executive who wants a more authentic way to lead or a spiritual person who wants to incorporate universal principles into your work, *The*

Zen Executive is an excellent guide to help bring out the best in your team, inspire the people you lead with genuine empathy, and harness those relationships to navigate the unknowns that lie ahead for all of us.

—Rev. Ken Daigle
Unity San Francisco, 2021

Table of Contents

Continued on next page

Introduction

Like so many, I came from humble beginnings. I grew up in the lower middle class, and my early family life was tumultuous to say the least. When I was 7, my father left my mother and me. We struggled mightily. It wasn't long before she met someone new, the man who would become my stepfather. He was retired from the Marine Corps after more than 20 years and had served three tours in Vietnam. Looking back, I can see that he suffered from undiagnosed PTSD for most of my formative years. Our relationship was one of soldier and commander. I was always kept in my place, and his idea of motivation was extreme verbal assault. Chores, discipline, and standards of perfection became my new reality. Anything less than perfection was met with damaging criticism and in some cases corporal punishment. This was my first experience of leadership—fear and intimidation.

Despite the unhealthy and dysfunctional upbringing, I was the first person in my family to go to college. I used a football scholarship to get an undergraduate degree in computer science, and while in college I was exposed to a world religions course. I had only ever experienced the Baptist form of Christianity, so this was an eye-opening experience for me. I was like a sponge. It was there I discovered that, at heart, I was a seeker.

I BEGAN TO
EXPERIMENT
WITH
LEADERSHIP
STYLES BASED
ON INSPIRATION,
KINDNESS, AND
COMPASSION.

Since then, I have spent my life searching for truth and wisdom in various religions, yoga, New Age modalities, and numerous Eastern philosophies. It was through this seeking that I began to see the array of universal truths found in all religions.

After college I went straight to work. I built a 20-year career in the tech industry and was blessed to work for some extraordinary organizations. During this time, I experienced many corporate cultures and various leadership styles. It turns out the seeker in me not only applied to my curiosity about life, God, and mysticism, but it drove me to study different leadership styles and approaches to culture building. It also motivated me to constantly seek improvement and evolution in my own performance and development. Once I entered leadership, I was on a quest to become the best leader possible. As a result of my commitment to constant evolution and improvement, I was afforded the opportunity to serve at some of the largest and most innovative and successful companies in the country.

More than anything during this time, I was a witness to cultures and leadership styles that mostly didn't work. They were more damaging than inspirational, and there was little regard for people or life outside of organizational success. These experiences coupled with my inner seeker left me wondering whether there was a better way. With each larger role I accepted, I began to experiment with leadership styles based on inspiration, kindness, and compassion as well as the overall well-being of those on my team. Many of those same themes ran through the ancient teachings I had studied all my life.

This book is a culmination of all that learning. I discovered there is a different way to lead and still have great success. There are areas where spiritual teachings and principles can overlap and lead us to great leadership and organizational success. We can lead from the heart and bring our spiritual path to work. Ultimately what began to drive me was to form a culture and leadership style that I would want to serve under, one that balanced people with a meaningful mission. After years of study, research, and practice, I have assembled in this book a few gems that I hope will help any leader who is looking for a better way to lead, one that uplifts people and increases performance but is also rooted in some of the most ancient spiritual traditions in the world.

After years in the tech industry leading teams as large as 200 people, I was given an opportunity for what I considered to be my dream job. A decade before, I had served as the chief information officer and vice president of operations for a large, spiritual nonprofit just outside Kansas City, Missouri. It is called Unity Village and serves as the world headquarters for Unity, part of a spiritual movement and philosophy that has several branches under the umbrella term *New Thought*. Unity was founded in 1889 by a husband and wife, Charles and Myrtle Fillmore, mystics who were way ahead of their time. Through their own miraculous healing stories, they began to form a set of teachings that would later become this global movement. They explored the nature of God and the universe in all world religions, assembling their learnings and teachings into a nondenominational philosophy that they began to share with others. This has culminated in a large 130-year-old publishing house, a cutting-edge prayer ministry based on affirmative prayer, and a stunning and sacred 1,200-acre campus. The campus is filled with Mediterranean-style architecture and amenities like a hotel, golf course, walking trails, fishing lakes, Airbnb cottages, and a magnificent 100-yard-long fountain in the central courtyard.

What I learned at Unity, both working there and studying the New Thought philosophy, has shaped and informed my leadership style. I want to tell you briefly about Unity teachings, not to convert you but so you will know where I'm coming from when I talk about spirituality in leadership.

New Thought teachings are for people who might call themselves "spiritual but not religious." It is for those who sense the depths of their own being and celebrate the awareness of a power greater than themselves.

The teachings in Unity bring together ancient wisdom with new interpretations of what it means to be alive and human. Unity inspires different ways to think about the force of love and intelligence that many people call God.

Some of what you'll find in Unity might sound familiar and other parts brand-new. Although the principles of healing and prosperity taught in Unity have now been scientifically explained, the ideas must have seemed radical a century ago.

Unity has no dogma. The Fillmores were reluctant even to issue a statement of beliefs. They wanted to remain in constant exploration. Throughout the years, they pulled together teachings of Truth that flow through all the world's great religions (thus the name Unity). Later, leaders of Unity boiled them down to five fundamental principles that are universal, meaning they apply to all people everywhere at any time.

The Five Principles

1. God/Source/the Universe is all there is and present everywhere. This is the force of love and wisdom that underlies all of existence.
2. Human beings are individual expressions of this underlying presence of the Divine and therefore inherently divine and good.
3. Thoughts have creative power to determine events and attract experiences.
4. Prayer and meditation keep us aligned with the one great power in the universe.
5. It is not enough to understand spiritual

> teachings. We must live the Truth we know by demonstrating and practicing these principles in our daily lives.

These basic principles gave me permission to see myself in a new way. By embracing myself as an expression of Source and learning to connect with this divine intelligence through prayer and meditation, I was able to transform years of embedded insecurities and lack of self-worth into feelings of worthiness and empowerment. A clear understanding of how our thoughts influence our experience of life helped me change my unproductive thoughts to those that were uplifting, supportive, positive, and productive. I had greater control (and responsibility) for how I was experiencing life. Using affirmations—positive statements focused on the outcome you seek—and other tools and resources, I began to heal some of the abuse and dysfunction I encountered in my youth.

Studying the works of Unity writers and teachers changed my life, so much so that I was compelled to attend the Unity seminary in a quest to achieve a Master of Divinity degree. This allowed me to feed the seeker within, while also serving in an executive capacity for this large and complex nonprofit.

Fast-forward a few years, and I had left Unity World Headquarters to pursue other opportunities in a couple of the most innovative and successful companies in the U.S. Then the CEO I had served under at Unity Village retired, and I was invited to apply for the role. This opportunity would open the door for me to implement across an entire organization the culture and leadership philosophies I had been cultivating and experimenting with in my various, more limited leadership roles. Many of the gems in this book come from the resulting success my leadership team and I have achieved using these new paradigms in leadership.

I finally did earn my Master of Divinity in 2020 from the Johnnie Colemon Theological Seminary and the next year was ordained a Unity minister. I have spent my career and life with one foot deeply rooted in seeking and learning spiritual truth and the other in corporate leadership, honing and sharpening my leadership skills. This book is a result of that journey and what I have learned along the way in merging the two paths.

The first half of my life, I thought of myself as a successful corporate guy who was deeply spiritual. What I have come to learn about myself with age, maturity, and wisdom is that I had it backward. I am a deeply spiritual man who has the gift of corporate leadership. This was a profound shift in how I viewed and understood myself. Truthfully, I am still learning to embrace this new realization even now. But this understanding has allowed me to accept and utilize my spiritual gifts and spiritual nature—and to value them just as much as I do my corporate leadership gifts. I have learned that it is not just one or the other but the combination of the two that has led me to experience success. The recognition (and acceptance) of this also created an opening for me to honor the balance of both. It offered me permission to feel whole and complete by integrating these two gifts into my identification of self. Throughout the remaining chapters you will find techniques and philosophies that merge head and heart so that we may lead and work from our fullest expression.

I have come to understand that any task can be made spiritual because our spirituality originates within our consciousness. We can bring a spiritual mindset or spiritual practices to any task, no matter how mundane or how pivotal. Strategy meetings can be spiritual. Contingency planning can be spiritual. Crafting a mission statement can be spiritual. Testing software can be spiritual. As I studied world religions and ancient teachings from around the globe, I began to see how easily their beauty and truth could be incorporated in—even function in alignment with—best business practices.

Throughout this journey I have continued to explore the spiritual principles I've learned throughout the years, and they have come to guide both my personal and professional lives. There is still tragedy, pain, and frustration to witness, and there is still a need to participate in the mechanics of running a large organization—managing the budgets, upgrading the technology, staying on top of deadlines. But there is an opportunity for us to face all of these realities of life with the knowledge that our thoughts create our experience and that we can find spiritual fulfillment even in our busy, modern lives. I have come to understand just how essential these practices for life are to creating career success, to being a leader of people, and to finding peace as a person.

PART ONE

An Inside Job

Making Money Is Permissible

Though there may be a natural tension between the application of spiritual practices or faith traditions and the adoption of corporate business best practices, the two can (and should) coexist. Marrying these two sides of the coin, especially in nonprofit organizations, leads to optimum performance; it makes prioritizing both organizational success and individual well-being possible.

The desire to succeed and to make money within a mission-driven and spiritually based organization is not wrong, corrupt, or even misguided. It is necessary to ensure the long-term sustainability of the organization and its sacred work in the world. If we step back and consider business best practices and metrics, it is most certainly the prioritization of profit over loss. However, a sole focus on profit as the primary measure of success can seem at odds with a nonprofit organization. Upon closer inspection, however, you will find that it isn't actually all about excess profit. The true desire of being "all about the money" for most organizations is simply to remain sustainable so the mission of the organization can continue. Becoming (and staying) profitable is a means to an end rather than the primary goal of the organization.

THE DESIRE
TO SUCCEED
AND TO MAKE
MONEY WITHIN
A MISSION-
DRIVEN AND
SPIRITUALLY
BASED
ORGANIZATION
IS NOT WRONG,
CORRUPT,
OR EVEN
MISGUIDED.

While I understand the centuries-old paradigm associating greed and corruption with money or profit, in reality money is simply a tool. It's the fuel that allows any organization to sustain and grow its mission. The Bible says it's the *love* of money that is the root of all evil; money itself is not bad, nor is making it. The issue here is the misdirected understanding that money means greed and corruption.

That's not the only stale and outdated assumption we make about money and spirituality. Another paradigm that remains embedded in our collective consciousness is the idea that you must be poor to be spiritual. In the past several decades, the pendulum has swung dramatically to the opposite extreme in some traditional faith systems with the emergence of the prosperity gospel, the idea that God blesses the faithful with wealth. Though this new tradition—and the increasing visibility and popularity of older prosperity traditions—have done much to dispel the idea that poverty is more spiritual, there is still an underlying current of this belief that feeds our social structure.

It is ironic to find this mental posture still in existence, although it shows up in public companies, nonprofits, ministries, and privately held institutions. I find this curious given the depth of prosperity and abundance teachings that have emerged in so many faith and religious traditions, both conservative and progressive, including Unity where I serve. Some of our greatest leaders, teachers, and founders assured us that wealth is acceptable, even desirable, in the spiritual realm. In a 1985 article in the *Chicago Tribune*, Rev. Dr. Johnnie Colemon said, "I go first class." She proclaimed, "Money is God in action. God is the source of my supply. I demonstrate the prosperity I teach about by having money in my pocket, money in my bank account, and material things. Nothing's wrong with money." Likewise, Unity cofounder Charles Fillmore wrote in his book *Prosperity*, "We shall serve for the joy of serving, and prosperity will flow to us and through us in streams of plenty."

Accordingly, the desire to employ business best practices within mission-driven organizations should not be met with criticism, fear, or harsh judgments. It's not a sign of greed, and it doesn't indicate a change in priorities, values, or mission. The long-term viability and success of any organization, whether for-profit or nonprofit, requires a dedicated commitment to excellence, hard work, honesty, and equity.

The truth is that defining a mission and values; remaining dedicated to diversity, equity, and inclusion; and engaging in modern and progressive business practices are crucial to organizations of all sorts—including ministries and spiritually based organizations—if they expect to achieve and maintain success.

I find it comforting, and even a sign of evolution, that so many businesses and ministries are adopting these practices in light of this deeper relationship. Perhaps the issue isn't with the adoption, implementation, and execution of best practices in a mission-driven organization, but rather with the false assumption that there is no heart, depth, or alignment of these practices with spiritual principle. Maybe a shift in consciousness, awareness, and the lens through which we view business best practices and the desire to make money is all that is needed to create a symbiotic relationship between business and the spiritual principles that guide our lives.

Tuning in to Intuition

A quick search on the internet will tell you that intuition is defined as "the ability to understand something immediately without the need for conscious reasoning," or "a thing that one knows or considers likely from instinctive feeling rather than conscious reasoning." For centuries, master teachers like Jesus, the Buddha, Lao Tzu, and more recently Charles and Myrtle Fillmore, Ernest Holmes, and others in the New Thought tradition have taught the value of connecting with our own innate intuition. Not only have they advocated for its value, but they have shared practical ways to find it, trust it, and incorporate it into transformational living. I would even venture to say it is a widely accepted concept and practice in most of

IT WAS TUNING IN TO MY GUT AND LISTENING TO THAT SMALL VOICE INSIDE THAT GUIDED ME TOWARD THE CHOICE I NEEDED TO MAKE.

the spiritual teachings in the world. Millions of people around the globe not only lean into their intuition for personal life decisions, but actually take conscious steps to develop and advance this skill to help improve their daily lives.

Yet this is an area where business and spirituality have diverged. Until very recently, intuition, if used in the business world at all, was certainly not talked about or recommended. In corporate circles, the decision-making ecosphere has largely been made up of three primary elements—facts, data, and the logic of the rational mind. Data is often relied upon in a variety of forms, including trends, surveys, and performance metrics. We want numbers to point to and analyze; we don't want to take a leap of faith. This lack of intuition, this refusal to acknowledge its value in all our affairs, is all too common in our society today, in which we tend to prioritize logic and rational thought above trusting our guts. Even to our detriment.

Fortunately, however, intuition is starting to make its way into corporate culture and people are starting to open their eyes to its powerful value. We are beginning to see corporate memes in mainstream social media with quotes like this one from Apple cofounder Steve Jobs: "Have the courage to follow your heart and intuition. They somehow already know what you truly want to become. Everything else is secondary." Or this one from Virgin Group founder Richard Branson: "I rely far more on gut instinct than researching huge amounts of statistics." Even the prolific media executive Oprah Winfrey touted the power of intuition when she said, "I've trusted the still, small voice of intuition my entire life. And the only time I've made mistakes is when I didn't listen." Books on intuition in the workplace, workshops and seminars on intuitive entrepreneurship, and even a surge in popularity for affirmational desk calendars or tarot decks and oracle cards for business and leadership all point to a shift in how we understand our work and make decisions. We're starting to realize that data and logic are important, but they're not the whole picture.

Developing and using our powers of intuition is more crucial today than maybe at any time in our history as leaders. In today's fast-paced world, the rate of change and the volume of information being produced, distributed, and consumed are at unprecedented levels—with no sign of diminishing. In much the same way that I recommend spiritual principles and business best practices can and should coexist, I feel the same about intuition and logic. We don't need to ignore data and facts in order to take advantage of our intuition. Nor should we. Relying on intuition alone can be a dangerous prospect when making big decisions, especially those that can have a major impact on entire organizations or communities. Instead, we have an opportunity to consider historical experience, all our personal learning, and the highest expression of our logical minds—and all the while we can lean into our innate, intuitive capabilities to make the best sense of a situation and discern how to move forward. In this way, business leaders can express and experience the best of both worlds—and become the best possible decision-makers.

In 2011, a colleague of mine from earlier in my career recommended me (unbeknownst to me) for a role at a global energy management company, a leader in the utility industry. I was surprised to get a call from their recruiter asking whether I was interested in a role overseeing their North American customer service operations, including a mission-critical data center that gathered data from tens of millions of electric, water, and gas meters from all over the U.S. on behalf of some of the largest utilities in the country. I had been serving as the chief information officer and vice president of operations at Unity for about five years at that point, and I hadn't been to a job interview in a few years. I thought I would go for the experience of it. Why not? It's what the business books tell us to do to "stay fresh." I didn't expect the experience to amount to anything because I was already in a good role and working toward a master's degree at a place I loved. There didn't seem to be any reason to make a change. But fast-forward a few weeks, and I was offered the role I'd only interviewed for on a whim.

I agonized over this decision. At the time, I was immersed in a dedicated meditation practice, so I took the decision into my meditation. I did this over and over and over. You may be wondering why I repeated this process many, many times. Why not sit down to think about it once and go with that? Because everything in the deepest part of myself was telling me to leave Unity and take this new role, while my mind and my heart were telling me to stay. Still struggling with my decision, and in a homiletics master's class where we learn the art of creating a sermon, I had the opportunity to hear a talk presented by a fellow student. The message of the talk was about how we create false ceilings for ourselves. We sometimes get comfortable and, either consciously or unconsciously, create these limits around what we can do or accomplish, whether related to our careers, our relationships, or even our money and prosperity. And there it was. Sitting in the back of that chapel, watching this burgeoning minister, I knew I had to follow the call to leave what had become a comfortable nest for me.

As I began this new role, the wheels in my mind were turning. In the spiritual environment of Unity and its broader community, everyone knew the value of meditation, contemplative prayer, and positive affirmations. We regularly opened and closed meetings with meditation or brief prayer. We used affirmations in our work, in our business planning, and even in our strategy. My spiritual practices and my business practices were intertwined in that world. How would I navigate the sterile and cold corporate environment, the command-and-control business world, and still honor what

THE BETTER
WE CARE FOR
OURSELVES
AND OUR WELL-
BEING, THE
BETTER WE CAN
PERFORM IN ALL
FACETS OF OUR
LIVES.

I now believed to be true: that spiritual practices and business practices could (even should) coexist?

After careful thought, I convinced myself that if I couched my messaging and practices in secular terms, I could use what I had learned at Unity in my new role. After all, my business gift, it seemed by now, was transformation and turnarounds. This would be the third turnaround effort in my career. In the interviews for this new role, I was told that the customer service team was struggling, that customers were not thrilled with the service levels, and that some fresh eyes and new life were needed to return it to the glory it once was. This was sure to be an interesting journey.

In the first few days of introducing myself to this team, I warned them we would be moving through a lot of change. Change in technologies, policies, procedures, and so on. As you can probably imagine, this was met with quite a bit of resistance. In an effort to help with the mental obstacle of being open to change, I introduced an affirmation to the group: *Change is our friend*. With every change I would ask the team to recite this message until the group began to embrace change.

I could tell very early on that I had made the right decision taking the job. This was a global leading company. They had more Ph.D.s on staff than I had ever seen in one place. The talent level was immense, and they knew how to innovate and how to develop products at a world-class level. They didn't realize it, but they oozed prosperity and abundance consciousness.

They had confidence and swagger. There was no challenge, no problem they didn't think they could overcome. There was no account they believed they couldn't win. They were using secular language yet affirming their way to success every single day. I saw it would be easy for me to integrate my own brand of spiritual practices into my work there, cloaked in secular language and slipped into teleconferences and PowerPoint presentations. That would be important because, in both my individual role and in my division, there was opportunity for improvement.

The division I was working with seemed to be showing cracks in the high-talent, high-success foundation the company was known for. Recent gaffes had caused the team to lose confidence in its work, and the folks who had been running this area prior to my arrival had little to no technology or IT experience. This division was almost exclusively an IT operation, and my years of IT experience would be the gift I brought to this operation.

Over the course of the next four or five years, we leaned into the affirmation: *Change is our friend.* During that time, we upgraded to state-of-the-art IT systems and practices, all while streamlining processes and procedures and implementing industry-standard methodologies for our operations. We stopped making assumptions about our work and sought new ways to accomplish the goals set before us. (Goals are a form of affirmation, but more on that later.) It is very easy, especially in large organizations, to stop questioning why we do something in a particular way or even why we do it at all. We get comfortable with "the way things are done" and assume that because we were successful before, there is no need to make a change. It was a perfect mirror for my own professional journey and my initial reluctance to even think about leaving my comfortable role at Unity. Embracing change proved to be successful both for me and my new team: The division was transformed, and I was promoted just 11 months into my new job.

When we tap into our intuition, it's common to bump into our feelings along the way. Choosing to focus on a broader understanding of our work is bound to do that. After all, considering a new choice or path, or simply going against the grain of what is expected of us (or what we think is expected of us), can stir up feelings of guilt, self-doubt, defensiveness, or fear. Having uncertainty or experiencing negative emotions, even in an otherwise positive situation, is a perfectly healthy human response. But it can be easy for us to get comfortable wherever we are in the moment, even in less-than-ideal circumstances. This is why it's so important to be prepared to acknowledge our feelings about certain decisions, projects, roles, or people—and not to let them become an obstacle.

It is particularly wise to be careful about holding grudges or getting caught up in past situations, which can cloud the intuition we worked so hard to tap into and which can inadvertently create an inability to move

ONE OF OUR GOALS AS LEADERS IS TO BE AT PEAK PERFORMANCE SO WE CAN MAKE BETTER DECISIONS AND BE AS PRODUCTIVE AS POSSIBLE.

forward. Our past experiences are not *this* experience, so we must remain open to what may be different in the scenario before us. For example, many of us have started new jobs in our lifetimes. After beginning a new gig, usually during the first few weeks, we meet a lot of people. Oftentimes, unsolicited, the people we meet will tell us about their coworkers. This sharing is based on one person's experience with another person, but their commentary can influence our thinking. I have heard new team members share their negative opinions about others, only to have a completely different experience with those folks myself. But the words of judgment indeed colored my expectations. In fact, even when my intuition was telling me someone was safe and trustworthy, my colleagues' judgment had me questioning my own intuitive feelings.

Another lesson I have learned is that we must at least be open to the possibility that people can grow and change. There have been countless times when I have had a terrible experience with a person. I would encounter them later and find myself leery of them, only to discover they were not the same person they were in our last encounter. They had learned from their mistakes, grown, and changed. Some of my most profound relationships have developed because I was willing to release old judgments about people and be open to seeing them anew. The same is true for events in our lives. When we experience a negative event, most of us will vow not to have that experience again.

Then in a few months or years, a replica scenario will arrive before us and trigger our memories of the bad experience. If we are not careful, our response to the present moment experience will be completely based on our historical perspective. The problem is we often miss the subtleties of how this experience is different and could work out differently. Because we are rooted in a historical perspective, we miss the opportunity for a new experience and often misjudge the reality of the current situation. The lesson here is to not let our historical perspectives and experiences color what our intuition is telling us but rather to trust it to guide us to something new and different.

When I received the job offer to leave a nonprofit and join a global corporation, looking at the facts alone couldn't give me the answer I needed. It was tuning in to my gut and listening to that small voice inside that guided me toward the choice I needed to make. My mind and heart were leading me to stay in my comfort zone at Unity. It was honoring that intuition, as difficult as it was at the time, that kept me moving forward on the path I was meant to be on.

In 2016 I returned to the nonprofit world, this time in the role of CEO. I came back to Unity Village with a wealth of experience and knowledge in product development, innovation, and the secrets of what it takes to be a global, leading organization. Unity, at age 130, was in need of exactly that type of support, and the tool kit has served me well as CEO. In hindsight, I can see clearly that honoring my intuitive promptings to leave gave me the knowledge and experience required to lead in this new capacity. I learned about the pillars of success in the halls of a global leader and tested my spiritual practices and intuitive decision-making skills in a corporate environment. The results of those experiences have been instrumental in our current successes at Unity, and I would have missed the opportunity had I not trusted my inner promptings.

Giving up People-Pleasing

As a leader who is interested in aligning professional success with spiritual principles, you are likely drawn to serving others, whether they are your associates or your congregants or your constituents. But serving others is not the same as tying yourself in knots to meet their expectations at any cost. Trying to meet others' expectations can result in feelings of pressure, stress, inadequacy, and even fear.

We all have ideas in our heads about how we are supposed to look or act or feel. That might not seem so terrible. After all, there are some standards of behavior we've agreed are for the good of society: not stealing, for instance, or not shouting "fire" in a movie theater. Where this can trip us up, however, is when the rules trickle down to all the different ways we show up in our day-to-day lives. Beyond those basic rules of decency, who is to say how we should work or socialize or dress? Many of us live in a sense of fear about what "they" will think or say about us. Who even is "they"?

Instead of guiding us toward a greater sense of well-being or a higher level of success, these unspoken standards we try to meet just lead to exhaustion. How often do you stop, change, or reconsider your hobbies, wardrobe, or lifestyle choices out of an unconscious (or conscious) worry about how someone else might perceive them? Even the smallest decisions end up based on a fear of what someone else might think. Ultimately, this can lead us to become consumed with resentment, frustration, and unhappiness. Not only does that make us feel miserable and stressed out, but it also has an impact on how we show up in the world and in our relationships.

Here is an important reminder: There is no collective "they" watching our every move. Sure, we have bosses who monitor us, and friends, colleagues, and family who observe us and sometimes judge us. However, it is not at the depth we are projecting, nor is it what we *think* they are thinking. The truth is most people are too caught up in their own personal concerns about how they fit in the world to be monitoring us at the levels we create in our minds. Furthermore, our objective on this journey is to honor *our* path, *our* truth, and *our* individual expression whether it agrees with the outside world or not. There is tremendous freedom in releasing all the fear associated with what other people will think because it allows us to be who we are without limitation or compromise. One of the secrets of this journey is that, ultimately, it really is all about us—our individual learning, development, and evolution. In the end, we're just experiencing and expressing our lives as the divine presence we were meant to be. When we can release the rest of it without regret and learn to embrace our own unique expressions, we find that being ourselves is a superpower.

Practicing the Four Pillars of Self-Care

When we strive toward being ourselves and becoming well-acquainted with our inner intuition, one of the best places to start is self-care. It can be tempting to write off self-care as a trend primarily related to spa days or a glass of rosé, but taking care of yourself is about much more than pampering. I can hear it already: "Jim, when do I possibly have time for something like self-care?"

But the question I want you to ask instead is, "What happens to us if we don't make the time to nurture our well-being?" Here's a hint: It's not good for us or anyone in our orbit, at home or on the job.

There have been times in my journey when I have burned the candle at both ends and put all my focus on my work. A few years ago, while working for the global leading organization, I was traveling about three weeks out of each month. I was consumed by deadlines and growth and the constant expectation for better results. Though I achieved some level of success in my role, it was at great expense to my life and my personal well-being. I was exhausted all of the time, the stress and the fear of failure were my only motivating factors, and I had little to no joy in my life. This didn't just affect me, of course. My wife felt as if she were the single parent of our young daughter, and I was emotionally unavailable to her. It put a tremendous strain on the most important relationship in my life. There was no joy because I was tired, irritable, and burned out most of the time. When I did find a few precious minutes of free time, I didn't feel like doing anything. My primary care physician reported that it was also taking a toll on my physical health in the forms of anxiety, sleep deprivation, dehydration, and an awful diet.

So I ask you, with these things unfolding within and around me, how could I ever have performed at my optimum level? The answer is simply that I could not. And the truth is that no one can. Here is the interesting dichotomy between self-care and putting in more hours to work harder: The fact is, the better we care for ourselves and our well-being, the better we can perform in all facets of our lives, from decision-making

WHAT HAPPENS TO US IF WE DON'T MAKE TIME TO NURTURE OUR WELL-BEING?

and planning for the future to how we react to stress and stimuli to how we show up in our relationships with our family and others.

How can we make self-care work for us? Let's define what self-care is really about and what it might look like for you. There are four pillars to ensuring that we are functioning at our absolute best. You will likely find each of these to be familiar, maybe even elementary. My goal is simply to remind you that these ideas are scientifically proven, and there are loads of case studies, research, and anecdotal data about the importance of each of them. I specifically include them in the book because one of our goals as leaders is to be at peak performance so we can make better decisions and be as productive as possible. Over the years I have found these pillars have a significant influence on performance in and out of the office.

1. Sweet Dreams

The first pillar, and maybe the most crucial, is sleep. Adults require seven to eight hours of sleep a night on average. No book, television show, news show, social media stream, or work (especially) should interfere with sleep. As important as these distractions might seem in the moment—and I know they can seem absolutely paramount to watch, hear, or do—none of them is as essential to your well-being as sleep.

Sleep contributes to better brain capabilities, improved mood, and increased immune system function. If your argument is that you are working late at night because it absolutely must be done, my rebuttal is that not only are you not doing your best work so late in the day, but you are setting yourself up for lackluster performance tomorrow. This can quickly become a vicious cycle that is difficult to break. Lack of sleep contributes to lesser overall mind and body function and dramatic mood swings as well as poor decision-making. Read that last part again. Prolonged lack of sleep leads to bad moods, bad decisions, and bad health. Need I say more?

2. Bon Appétit

The next pillar is food. A healthy diet is not one-size-fits-all and can often feel like a moving target. What works for one person is not necessarily the right choice for someone else. What works for you in the middle of winter may not work so well in the heart of summer. Your ideal diet can also shift as you age, if you change your exercise habits, or when you are dealing with short- or long-term health concerns.

Still there are some good general rules of thumb to follow, including prioritizing real food and eating at least three times daily. Eating plenty of fruits and vegetables and getting enough macronutrients (fats, proteins, and carbohydrates) is important for everyone—even if it looks a little different from plate to plate. Focusing on whole foods is a good place to start. Foods that are factory-produced or highly processed often contain chemicals and additives that mess with our moods and impact our brain function, decision-making, and sleep patterns. And don't forget the water! We are, after all, about 80 percent water, so it is important to stay hydrated to keep our systems functioning at their highest level.

3. Get Moving

The third pillar is exercise (I can hear you booing me). Any kind! You don't have to become a marathon runner or register for a triathlon to practice self-care through exercise. We have a tendency to want to take the big strides rather than the baby steps, but a little movement every day goes a much longer way than a strenuous workout every once in a while. Walking, yoga, and dancing around the house (or even in your office chair) are all great ways to incorporate movement in your day. Household chores, from vacuuming to dusting to folding laundry, can also help you get your heart rate up.

Like diet and sleep, regular movement has a ripple effect through other facets of life, including many long-term benefits. Exercising can help you get to sleep faster and stay asleep longer. It can help your body better manage blood sugars. Movement can strengthen muscle and bone, and it can reduce your risk of anxiety and depression. Exercise releases endorphins, the powerful mood enhancers that bring stress relief and contribute to a general feeling of well-being.

4. The Spiritual Side

Of course, self-care isn't only about our physical well-being. Though we rely on healthy bodies to get the most out of our lives and our work, there's a fourth pillar to the foundation we're building. The ancient teachings are clear: Life is an inside-out experience. We are each a unique and divine expression of Spirit. But when we neglect our spiritual side, we can feel out of sorts and at our wit's end before we even show up to our daily tasks or passion projects. If we are not in a healthy place with our internal thoughts and feelings, all the self-care in the world will not bring us peace.

Minimizing unrest, suffering, and turmoil in our experience of life begins within. Make it a priority to reconnect with your spiritual practice on a regular basis, ideally daily. Make meditation a habit, engage (or reengage) with a prayer practice, or commit to a journal. Attend a church service, read a religious text, or participate in a devotional. Have a conversation with a spiritual or religious leader, a therapist or counselor, or a close friend. Honoring our spiritual nature can help us connect with an inner strength and sense of well-being, helping us express the best version of ourselves as we move about our world.

Staying Committed to Yourself

Many of us have been teaching, preaching, and serving others using these techniques for years. It can feel simple, even obvious, to tell our coworkers, congregants, and loved ones to take it easy on themselves, to prioritize their own health and well-being. But what about ourselves? It may feel as if we're being selfish or greedy to take that time to focus on our own needs, but it's true what they say: You can't pour from an empty cup. If we don't provide for our own wellness, it limits our capacity to serve others. Reminding ourselves of that truth can help us see those "selfish" choices as a sign of our self-awareness or even self-acceptance. An aversion to appearing greedy isn't the only common roadblock to self-care. We may also ignore these pillars simply because they seem too basic. "Well, *of course*, I should get a good night's rest," you might say as you move on to the next item on your to-do list instead of putting yourself to bed.

In committing to these four pillars, you won't believe how much better you will feel every day. Consider what happens when we neglect them: Lack of sleep causes poor mental function and altered mood, which usually manifests as crankiness, a short temper, and poor decision-making. The same holds true with lack of food or poor diet. In fact, a diet lacking in proper nutrition has been proven to have the same or even worse side effects as not eating at all.

So please, get your rest, stay hydrated, and exercise a few times a week. Honor your own divinity. Be mindful of what you consume, including the food you put in your body and the media you engage with (and when). It really does make a difference and will help provide a good foundation for your days, ensure your mood and biological systems are stable and consistent, and help your mental function.

While these steps are critical to ongoing self-care, we still must go further to ensure our overall health and wellness. Plus, it doesn't hurt to give ourselves an extra treat now and then. Sure, that spa day would be nice, but it doesn't have to take a lot of time or expense to push your self-care to the next level. Find something outside your day-to-day routine that will help you rejuvenate and bring a sense of renewal. Often the intention behind it is more important than the thing itself. Go play a round of golf, take yourself to an afternoon movie, turn off your phone, and pick up that novel. My personal rule is to do something for my own rejuvenation and renewal every four to six weeks. That is about the maximum amount of time I can go in full-on execution mode before I need a day to just let go and exhale and take a break. Part of being the best version of yourself, both at work and at home, requires a committed focus on taking care of yourself. You probably won't ever look

FIND SOMETHING OUTSIDE YOUR DAY-TO-DAY ROUTINE THAT WILL HELP YOU REJUVENATE AND BRING A SENSE OF RENEWAL.

back on years gone by and say to yourself that you wish you had worked more. However, you likely already find yourself wishing for better sleep, more fun in your days, and a healthier lifestyle. Science tells us that the healthier we are, the better we perform in every aspect of our lives. Now is the time to embrace change and make yourself a priority!

Motivational author Louise Hay said, "Wellness is the natural state of my body," and she's exactly right. Instinctively, the body's desired state is one of perfect health and wellness. We see this every day when our immune system automatically kicks into gear to overcome a cold, when a cut immediately starts to clot then heal itself, and when our bruises melt away without deliberate intervention. We are constantly in a state of moving toward healing and well-being, no matter what we do. But, like most things, when we align our thoughts and intentions and actions with wellness in mind, we can experience even greater outcomes. Science tells us that the living cells in our bodies respond directly to our thoughts, words, and visualizations, so let's leverage that. We can use that knowledge to transform our physical experience and promote a better all-around experience of our life and work.

Still, our bodies don't always move at the pace we wish they would. This is where patience—and having great compassion for ourselves—is key. Everything is cyclical and paying attention to our own patterns and needs can help us ensure the self-care work we're doing is as effective as possible. Getting frustrated that you don't have the mental clarity to finish a task before the end of the day or running yourself ragged in the run-up to a major event is not congruent with a healing atmosphere. While it may feel as if you're getting ahead by plowing through your own "check engine" light warnings, you're likely putting yourself even further behind in the long run. When we're not feeling our best, we're probably not doing our best.

This is a tough lesson to learn, particularly for leaders who want to set an example of dedication and commitment to organizational objectives—not to mention your personal aspirations—and for those of us with a service mentality, who are eager to give of ourselves to our families, teams, and communities. But the bottom line is we must learn to honor our own needs if we want to create internal peace that can be shared with others. Practice accepting how you feel without guilt or judgment, practice setting healthy boundaries, and you will find yourself so much healthier, mentally, emotionally, and even physically. Just note the word above—*practice*. That means it might take us a while to become consistent in forming these good habits. Let us not beat ourselves up when we have a setback but rather let it serve as a reminder for next time, knowing we will do better so we can be better.

Sometimes we resign ourselves to fatigue and stress, or even to burnout and anxiety, but it doesn't have to be that way. Remember your intuition. We can be quick to disregard that still, small voice inside, but it is almost always right. Whether your instinct is to say *yes* to that new position or decline it, to soldier on through your block of work time or to pause and take a nap, or to hit the gym for a tough workout or to finally crack open that novel—trust it. When we force ourselves to do things out of a sense of obligation and deny our instincts, it won't be long until we run into trouble. That's not to say we can ignore the trash that needs taking out or the organizational budget that needs to be cut in order to maintain solvency. There will always be tough things we'd rather not do. But if the less-delightful parts of life will always be there, no matter which path we're on, we should also take advantage of every opportunity to choose what resonates instead of something we feel obligated to pick. Living life this way offers enthusiasm and contentment, not resentment and stress.

To be the best version of ourselves in whatever we are doing, we need to make ourselves a priority and take time for physical and mental care. Our entire sense of well-being depends on our commitment to self-care. What happens if we don't prioritize self-care? We begin to take on more stress. Resentment can start to build up. Overwhelming feelings of burnout, depression, or lack of appreciation can take over, and that can lead to neglecting the four pillars—and then to a snowball effect of poor self-care. These breakdowns in the system can begin to affect all aspects of our lives: the quality of our work, the quality of our rest, and the quality of our relationships with coworkers, our loved ones, and our interactions with the general public.

There is a powerful connection between rest, diet, physical health, and spiritual well-being and how we show up in the world. Do yourself and those around you a big favor: Practice great self-care! You won't regret it, and neither will they.

Meditating Really Is Worth Your Time

I'm guessing you often find yourself thinking that you'd like to get more done—during the day and in life—and that you wish you were less stressed. I bet your associates feel the same way. Believe it or not there is a way we can accomplish both, and it sort of involves doing nothing. We just have to do nothing in a particular way.

There are, of course, seemingly endless ways we're told we can increase our productivity while reducing stress, which usually tend to exacerbate rather than improve the problem. So try to forget the Top 10 lists and consider this one ancient and simple change for easing the pace of life and allowing yourself to be more productive every day, no matter how motivationally challenged you might be. This single practice is likely

IT SEEMS PARADOXICAL TO THINK YOU CAN SLOW DOWN FOR A FEW MINUTES A DAY TO BECOME HEALTHIER AND MORE PRODUCTIVE, BUT IT IS TRUE.

to elicit some groans because it seems counterintuitive and is easy to avoid by making excuses. Are you ready for me to unveil this ancient secret of productivity and creation? I will do so with an old Zen proverb: You should sit in meditation for 20 minutes every day. Unless you're too busy, in which case you should sit for an hour.

That's right, friends, sitting completely still in silence or listening to a guided meditation or simply peaceful music is the secret to getting more done in your life. Look, I didn't believe it either. It did not make sense to me. But when I began this practice years ago, I was a young executive with crushing responsibility, trying to earn my master's degree at the same time. Fortunately, I was deeply entrenched in a network of people who believed in this sort of thing, and I was convinced to give it a try. Researching the scientific perspective, I learned that silence really is the secret. Why? For starters, meditation reduces stress and helps control anxiety. It improves concentration and boosts memory retention. It increases feelings of acceptance, kindness, and happiness, not to mention your self-awareness and self-esteem. It slows signs of aging, reduces blood pressure, and benefits cardiovascular and immune health. You get all that from sitting in silence? *Yes*.

I had done the research on meditation, but I still didn't expect what came next. Like most, I was constantly feeling overwhelmed by the pressure of things that needed to be done—professionally, in school, and in my personal life. I began a simple 5- to 10-minute practice of sitting in silence each morning. I did it very consistently. (Consistency is the absolute key to success for this.) Within a few days, my life began to change even beyond all those benefits I just listed. The more I meditated and the more I relaxed, the less worry I carried and the less I struggled. Life somehow became easier to navigate. My to-do lists were accomplished with ease, and my life was much less tumultuous.

Meditation is the art of relaxing the body and quieting the mind. When quieting the mind, you are clearing out excessive thoughts, many that are critical and negative. By clearing the mind, we remove the resistance that keeps us from creating what we really want. We open up to clarity, inspiration, intuition, ideas, and opportunities that will serve our goals and desires rather than undermine them. Without the negative chatter, you will be amazed at how much clarity you gain. It seems paradoxical to think you can slow down for a few minutes a day to become healthier and more productive, but it is true. Elementary schools, first responders, and organizations of all types and sizes around the world are now incorporating meditation practices into their daily routines with incredibly beneficial results.

Really, you don't have time *not* to meditate. It doesn't have to take 20 minutes. Just begin by being grateful for a few things, then sit in silence for five minutes. Start there and see where it grows.

Many people feel intimidated by meditation, picturing a strict practice that requires skill or training. But there truly is no right way to meditate; there are thousands of techniques you can use. Start simple with something that works for you, remembering that the practice differs from person to person. Focus on your breath going in and out, and just feel what you feel. Gently observe your thoughts with no judgment. Practice noticing them but not engaging with them. Remind yourself that there's no need to try to be perfect. When you realize you're caught in a thought or a worry or a memory, simply let it go and start again. Relax in the moment.

The most important part is this: Be consistent. Make it a priority. Meditation must come first to make it a new habit. Try adding a few minutes of meditation to a daily habit you've already established: Meditate for two minutes after you brush your teeth, or for five minutes while you wait for coffee to brew, or for 10 minutes after you've put the kids to bed. Starting this way, you can create a meditation practice that will bring more peace and better health, with greater clarity and productivity.

When—not if—you realize the benefits of a meditation practice, this can be a great tool to bring to your organization. You don't have to put group meditation sessions on everyone's calendar in order to promote the benefits of spending a little time in silence. Consider sharing your own practice with your team. Normalize taking breaks to sit outside on a bench or in the break room outside of the lunch hour. We often succumb to the pressures of needing to be productive constantly. Make it acceptable to take a few minutes throughout the day simply to breathe. You'll be amazed at the positive effects that can ripple out from this one simple habit.

Dropping the Baggage

Our inner work and self-care practices are just that—a practice—not onetime conversations or occasional activities like feel-good workshops. Sooner or later, despite our best efforts, we will each have experiences that lead to feelings of self-doubt, inadequacy, insecurity, and fear. Too often we ignore these feelings by pressing them down or attempting to put a positivity bandage on them. Avoidance will only lead to a cycle of repetition, making it difficult to stop. Instead, we must have the courage to look at our pain, our sorrow, and our trauma—and the feelings that result—without letting them define us.

Through our inner work and self-care practices, we can learn how to see our difficult circumstances and negative feelings as separate from ourselves. Experiencing fear does not make us fearful and feeling inadequate doesn't make us inadequate. Let us learn to take from them the understanding of how to live with them in ways that can take us higher or transcend them completely.

Depending on your life experience, your feelings of inadequacy or unworthiness may have been born from a critical parent or abusive relationship. To this day I am still unraveling the repeated messages I received in my formative years about my abilities, my body, and whether I would "amount to anything." My path to healing was born out of becoming clear that just because someone said it—and I still hear that voice or those words in my head—does not mean *I am that*. In fact, I most certainly am not what they told me, but I had to become willing to see myself as I am and not what was projected upon me. I had to become willing to define my own story and lean away from the lens of others. It is in that work that I have been able to heal and transcend those struggles.

In the same way, fear is natural; we just don't want to live there. I have met countless professional speakers, leaders, athletes, and entertainers who, even after years of perfecting their craft, still have moments of fear. Many have learned to feel the fear, understand it is part of the process, and move right through it. Others told me that instead of calling it fear or nervousness, they have learned to "rebrand" their emotions and physical responses as excitement to create a more positive experience. Being open to our feelings, coupled with a willingness to explore them, work to discover the source, and take steps to see them in a new light, can put us on the path toward healing.

This isn't only for the benefit of our mental health. Emotions, feelings, and reactions all have an impact on the cells and systems of our physical bodies, meaning that cultivating inner peace not only supports our mental acuity but also contributes to overall well-being.

When we are facing a disturbance—a stress of some kind—our emotions may get the better of us. We can slip into feelings of anger, upset, or anxiety. We may tense our bodies, use poor language, experience increased blood pressure or heart rates, and have all sorts of negative thoughts that spin uncontrollably in our minds. A single event can upset our physical bodies and also make us grumpy and resentful for an entire day. How many of us have started our day alert and generally positive only to receive some frustrating news or have something happen—like spilling coffee all over the presentation you were about to share with a client? I know I have. And unfortunately, in the past I have carried that anger and frustration with me right into the office or my next activity. I have snapped at undeserving coworkers or family members and made poor decisions that I later regretted, all because my frame of mind was not in the right place.

Consider that for a moment. How many decisions will we make from this cranky, angry place? Would we make different choices if we were deciding from a happy place? Some decisions may not have much of

THE TEST IS ALWAYS TO BE OPEN TO HEARING WHAT IS BEING SAID WITHOUT GETTING DEFENSIVE OR BEING PULLED INTO A POWER STRUGGLE TO BE "RIGHT."

an impact while others could be catastrophic if made hastily or from anger. In addition, consider how often we find ourselves mired in negative emotions. What is the collective impact of our poor decision-making? The way we approach all our choices, day in and day out, can change our experience of the day, our life, and the lives of others. Just as the flap of a butterfly's wings can cause a typhoon, so can our myriad choices have a ripple effect far beyond our imagination.

How can we intervene, then? Psychotherapist Viktor E. Frankl is credited with saying, "Between stimulus and response there is a space. In that space is our power to choose our response. In our response lies our growth and our freedom." Often, we are moving so quickly in thought and word that we skip right past this space. But if we catch it, we have an opportunity in that space to choose from a calmer place. We can accept this unfolding and be open to the possibility that everything can still work in a perfect way—even though it may not be what we expect in the moment. This is where we are called to trust the process. This puts us in a better position to care for ourselves and in a clearer state for how we can respond or provide support to others.

Serving as CEO in an innovative culture where we have created change both internally and customer-facing, I have had a fair number of phone calls from the Unity faithful and a handful of customers who were not in favor of some of our changes. These delicate conversations are the perfect environment to practice pausing and centering prior to responding. As you might imagine, some of these calls can be quite critical, so the test is always to be open to hearing what is being said without getting defensive or being pulled into a power struggle to be "right."

With time I have been able to look back and see that when I became present, I could listen deeply without becoming defensive, and in almost every case, there was a nugget of wisdom that we could use to improve what we were doing. I would also say that the mere effort to listen thoughtfully to people and their grievances is all that is needed, even when you end up not agreeing. Most people are like all of us—they just want to be seen, heard, and acknowledged. Because I have learned this, I return every phone call or email, every letter or inquiry I receive. The fact that people are reaching out means they still care, and the act of showing that you care by listening to them can deepen the relationship.

We can't control all of life, but we don't have to feel powerless either. No matter what happens, it is our response to circumstances that shape our experience. The foundational component of better living is managing our thoughts, emotions, and perceptions. The more in touch we become with our thoughts, emotions, and perceptions, the more clarity we will have to manage and change them, for both short- and long-term benefit. Allowing ourselves to feel our emotions fully does not mean that our thoughts (and therefore our perception of life) become fearful, negative, and worrisome. Minimizing the disturbances we experience helps us have healthier bodies, make better decisions, and show up as our best selves in our organizations and communities.

Taming the Inner Critic

It's often our own self-talk that trips us up, not external factors and circumstances, and that negative inner voice can lead to detrimental effects. Sadly, many of us remain unaware that we are indeed our own harshest critic. We move through our days with an endlessly chattering mind—and much of the time it is blathering on about us! It is judging how we look, what we should or should not have said, whether we are in the right job, the right house, the right relationship, and on and on. You name it and we have an internal opinion about it, and it is usually overblown and out of touch with the reality of the situation.

This may not even be our own voice. If we grew up in a household with critical parents, relatives, or siblings, we may hear one of their voices and not even realize it. In fact, recent psychology suggests that with the death of a critical parent, adult children struggle mightily with the grieving process because of a profound sense of relief combined with a tremendous sense of guilt and shame for feeling freed and relieved—all without much understanding of these feelings. Fortunately for some, guided professional grief counseling navigates them through those emotions, ultimately allowing them to focus solely on grieving the actual loss of the parent.

So why is it important that we manage this critical voice if we all have one? This negative self-talk and negative thinking has an impact, a ripple effect. It can cause us to put needless pressure on ourselves, and it can also increase feelings of anxiety, fear, anger, and, if left unchecked, even depression. For example, how many times have you left a meeting or a social situation where you felt as if you had really blundered and were terribly embarrassed, only to have your friends, coworkers, or others barely remember the situation? This is the power of our inner critic. It has an extraordinary memory and a unique ability to poke at our most vulnerable thoughts and feelings. Something we created in our minds as a mountain turns out to be barely an anthill. Think about the minutes, hours, or sometimes days of energy, emotion, and stress that we put into these scenarios—we can find ourselves spinning from the anxiety and fear created by the negative self-talk—even when everything turns out just fine.

I can remember my own inner dialogue prior to accepting the CEO role at Unity. The organization had been relatively stagnant for several years and many of its offerings were in a downward decline. Many times, in considering my application for the role, my own inner critic had me questioning my ability to make a difference where other leaders had struggled. Had I listened solely to this fear-based mental chatter, I might have missed one of the best opportunities in my career. Instead, I changed my focus to all the wonderful opportunities for innovation and change. This shifted my mental posture from one of trepidation to one of optimism and enthusiasm.

Even as we commit to something as simple as a morning workout routine or a healthier diet or a new mindfulness practice, we catch ourselves skipping a step or missing a day and the inner critic starts in—often leading to a complete abandonment of the initial effort over one perceived mistake. We end up back at square one over and over again, feeling more and more discouraged every time.

So what can we do to better manage the mental chatter of the inner critic? First, be deliberate about observing your thinking, and become aware of this inner voice. Some experts advocate giving it a silly name to add some levity. After all, it is hard to take the inner critic seriously when it has a name like Negative Nellie or Toxic Tom.

A meditation practice can be a great way to help you notice your inner critic and work to manage its chatter so you can get some peace. Once you become aware of it, you have a few different options for responding to it. Start asking yourself whether you would talk to a friend this way in the same situation. If not, what would you

NEGATIVE SELF-TALK CAN CAUSE US TO PUT NEEDLESS PRESSURE ON OURSELVES AND INCREASE FEELINGS OF ANXIETY, FEAR, ANGER, AND EVEN DEPRESSION.

say to that friend instead? Whatever you would say to a friend is what you should be saying to yourself. You can also stop the spiral of supercritical thinking by naming your negative or critical thoughts and asking whether this is the ultimate truth—or whether it's possible to see it differently.

In almost every case, if we are responding from our highest self and not from emotion, we will be directed to a higher level of thinking that results in liberation from the problem that sent us down the spiral in the first place.

Sometimes our inner critic shows up because it's trying to protect us from something. Ask your critic what it's trying to keep you safe from—whether that's looking foolish in front of the boss (so it chimes in to remind you of that silly thing you said in the last meeting in hopes you'll be less likely to speak up this time) or getting your heart broken (so it belittles or shames you when you're getting ready for a date that you'd been really excited about the day before). Remind your inner critic that risk is a part of life and there's no need to panic.

Remember that not every problem the inner critic imagines is actually looming large and dangerous. Simply taking a step back and examining the reality of the situation can help identify the actual size of the problem, and be completely confident in how you move forward in dealing with it if it needs to be dealt with.

Do not forget that perfection is not the goal, even when our critic thinks perfection is a reasonable objective. We can stop holding ourselves to ridiculously high standards that no human can possibly meet. Adherence to perfection is simply not a standard we demand of anyone else in our reality, yet we seem to expect it of ourselves. We must learn to embrace our own imperfections with compassion and understanding and at the same time balance that with the will to do better as we become more aware.

Becoming aware of the inner critic and maintaining at least some semblance of control over it will most certainly put us on a path to a more peaceful existence. This will help us achieve a happier and healthier life as we navigate an already complex world. No need to beat ourselves up along the way! May we find the compassion and patience for ourselves that we would feel for a child who is learning and growing, because we are learning and growing.

Moving Forward in Forgiveness

If you are like me, there are times I read a phrase like "forgiveness and the art of well-being" and immediately bristle with resistance. Why? Because sometimes there are fresh events in my life where I might still be holding raw energy or emotions, and I am not ready to embrace the idea of forgiveness. Then I force myself to remember the most important but often unrealized aspect of forgiveness. For many, forgiveness feels like a sacrifice or concession that lets someone off the hook. It feels like an act we are being asked to perform for the benefit of making someone else feel better. What I would like you to consider with me now is that the act of forgiveness is something extremely powerful that we do for *ourselves* and not another person.

Allow me to explain. First and foremost, when we need to forgive someone, we typically have stored energy or emotion around this event or person. We may be carrying anger, hurt, or resentment, and each time we think of that circumstance, we relive the incident. In doing so, we rekindle all the original emotions, which can create stress in our minds, hearts, and even bodies.

I want to be sensitive to the pain associated with these past events. The events were real, in some cases even traumatic. We are human beings, and emotion is a significant part of our experience. It is important to allow ourselves to acknowledge our emotional pain and trauma, to feel our feelings deeply and without judgment, so we can process them in a healthy way rather than stuff the feelings. That said, our goal in feeling and processing these emotions is to move past them so we won't become stuck in the anger or pain or resentment. Our tendency is often either to ignore our feelings, not allowing ourselves to experience them at all, or to feel them so intensely that we can't let them go. We must try to find the middle path.

Remembering past events that upset us can be mood-altering. The resurrection of a memory can affect our mental and emotional state as well as our mood because of the emotions it conjures up. Often, we end up taking it out on the world around us days, weeks, months, or even years after the original act. It can also affect our decision-making and choices well into the future. This is why the act of forgiveness can free us.

Forgiveness is an act of self-care that can free us from recalling an experience and regenerating its painful emotions. We can stop the pattern and its impact on our minds, bodies, and emotional state. We can cease the roller coaster and its harm to ourselves. This is how we move past these emotions, prioritizing our own sense of well-being and promoting better decision-making skills. Once we are able to release our mental and emotional processing of the past, we open our minds and hearts to current circumstances. We choose to fill the space with gratitude and focus on the positive desires and outcomes we are seeking in the present moment.

We must remember to include ourselves in this practice, to forgive ourselves for things we might consider mistakes or wrong choices. This is often more powerful than forgiving others. It is very easy to hold on to all of our worst decisions or management mistakes, hindering our leadership and decision-making abilities before we've even begun. To release ourselves from the

FORGIVENESS IS AN ACT OF SELF-CARE THAT CAN FREE US FROM RECALLING AN EXPERIENCE AND REGENERATING ITS PAINFUL EMOTIONS.

bondage of our past actions is every bit as beneficial as forgiving another. Once we have forgiven ourselves, we can begin anew—without the shadows of previous problems or complications hanging over us.

That's all fine and good, you might be thinking. *But I can't just forgive someone (or myself) with the snap of my fingers.* If you are unsure how to embark on your forgiveness journey, I have a mantra that I found years ago and use to this day. Anytime I have a memory or disturbance I want to release, I become still and bring to mind the person or circumstance. Then I recite the following:

> ***For whatever harm I have caused others, may they forgive me.***
>
> ***For whatever harm others have caused me, may I forgive them.***
>
> ***For whatever harm I have caused myself, I forgive myself.***

Depending on the magnitude of what I am trying to forgive, I might have to repeat this practice several times to release all my energy about the situation. But without fail, after repeating this practice a few times, I notice the energy dissipates and I am able to release the experience and free myself from the past. This work is critical to our own health and well-being, and also to promoting a spirit of patience, compassion, and appreciation in our organizations.

Gems from Part One: An Inside Job

- It's okay to make money. Money is the fuel that allows any organization to sustain and grow its mission. Being poor is *not* more spiritual than having money, and there is nothing wrong with a healthy prosperity focus.

- The value of using intuition is growing in the business world, and it's more crucial today than ever. Facts and data are important but only part of the picture. What do you know deep down?

- Believe your own intuition and experience rather than letting the opinions of others cloud your judgment.

- People can grow and change. Stay present and give them a chance to be better than they used to be.

- It's exhausting to try to live up to what "they" might think. Honor your path, your truth, and your individual expression.

- Nurture your own well-being. Making time for self-care will improve every aspect of your life, including your performance and decision-making at work.
- Pay attention to the four facets of self-care: Get enough sleep, eat a healthy diet, get some exercise, and connect with a spiritual practice every day.
- You are not selfish for taking care of yourself. Everyone around you will be better off if you are rested, healthy, clearheaded, and in touch with your inner spirit.
- Meditate. Just do it. The time is minimal and the benefits are enormous.
- Do your inner work. Feelings of fear, unworthiness, or inadequacy can make you sick, upset, miserable, and damage your relationships at work and home. Be willing to explore what might be holding you back.
- Pause in the space between stimulus and response. Most people just want to be seen, heard, and acknowledged. Show you care by listening without being defensive.
- Be aware of your own self-talk, the critical inner dialogue that discourages you from reaching for the stars. The inner voice can be wrong and often comes from fear. There are ways to manage it.

♦ Forgiveness is something we do for ourselves. Pain and anger from the past can overwhelm the present and dominate today's decisions. Release yourself from bondage, whether you're forgiving another person or yourself.

PART TWO

Mission Critical

Identifying Your Mission

We're learning how to trust our intuition when it comes to our own personal or professional decision-making, but how do we check in with the inner voice of an organization? This is the importance of having a clear mission and an explicit value statement because it offers a guiding light when we face difficult choices, big decisions, or questions of priority.

Before we can identify how to develop such guidance, we must make sure we're clear about what we want that guidance to help us attain. Like so many things, we need to answer the *why* before we can answer the *how*. If you haven't identified the true *why* behind your organization, it's going to be very difficult to create a meaningful mission statement or to highlight the values that matter most. Just setting your sights on being the biggest or the best is a hollow mission that can easily be tripped up when your team faces obstacles or if your intentions are thwarted by factors outside your control. If your team is facing an important question and turns to organizational guidance that merely says, "Be the best," that isn't likely to help very much. We need to know what specific end we're seeking.

As author and speaker Simon Sinek says, "The *why* is the purpose, cause, or belief that drives every one of us." I'm reminded of someone who once asked, "When you leave your house in Kansas City in the morning, what keeps you from ending up in Alaska?" We rarely give much thought to how many intentions, goals, and objectives keep us on a path each and every day. Without them, who knows where we might end up at the end of the day. The same is true for businesses, nonprofits, and any organization of people. We must have a common destination in mind that drives everything else we do.

The truth is, becoming "the best" at anything is a difficult mission to achieve because it relies on others *not* making the mark as much as it depends on your organization exceeding expectations. It may be worth setting those types of lofty goals to help you achieve your mission, but the why-focused mission and the deeper meaning behind your work are what's at the heart of your success—not the growth metrics or the glowing reviews. It is that heart that gives people the opportunity to connect with you, whether they're your employees, your investors, or your customers. And if you want to build loyalty among your staff and get buy-in from your audience, you'll need the ability to connect.

"People don't buy what you do; they buy why you do it," Sinek says in his popular TED Talk "How Great Leaders Inspire Action." "And what you do simply proves what you believe."

That last part is important, too, because what we're ultimately seeking with a mission statement is alignment. Putting a mission statement on your website or your

HOW WE EXPERIENCE LIFE DEPENDS ON WHAT WE THINK ABOUT THOSE THINGS THAT ARE OCCURRING BEFORE US, NEAR US, AND TO US.

walls without acting accordingly leaves those words empty and meaningless. If what you're doing doesn't prove what you believe, no elaborate mission statement is going to fix that gap. Developing a meaningful mission statement based on your *why* isn't always easy work, even if the direction seems simple. It often takes real work and focus to drill down to the primary driver behind *why* you do *what* you do.

So, *how* do we do that? Let's begin with what might be the most important (and maybe the most challenging) practice: getting inside your own head. You may be wondering what your own thoughts have to do with your organization's mission. You might even be thinking, *Jim, life does not happen inside my head; life is what occurs on the outside.* True, but how we experience life depends on what we think about those things that are occurring before us, near us, and to us. We witness what is happening then form our thoughts and judgments almost instantaneously.

The mind is the generator of the seemingly endless voice we hear in our heads every day all day. Since we are all much more than our minds, we can actually choose to observe these thoughts or change them to something completely different. Try it right now. Instead of thinking, *Jim has really lost it*, reread the last few sentences and immediately change your thoughts to, *I understand what he is saying, and I can change my thoughts that quickly!* See? You did it!

Are you still wondering why we're doing this? There is a popular saying, "Your mind is a garden; your thoughts are the seeds. You can grow flowers, or you can grow weeds." It is always a good time to begin the practice of tending to the garden of our minds, especially when we're endeavoring to create something meaningful out in the world. Just as we depend on our thoughts to create our reality and drive our experience of life, a mission statement helps create our organization's reality and drive how each of our stakeholders—whether internal or external—interacts with it.

Finding Your Calling

Today millions of people have jobs or roles that are unfulfilling, sometimes woefully so. You might be thinking, *Yeah, so? No one really likes their job.* To which I reply: That doesn't make it okay! Consider for a moment the profound impact of spending the majority of your time in a role that is ungratifying. Every day it is affecting your mood. Every day it is causing mental and physical stress, negative thinking, and a habit of dissatisfaction. If you don't find any fulfillment at work, those feelings can build to despair and seep into all the facets of life.

IT IS POSSIBLE, EVEN PREFERABLE, TO HAVE A JOB THAT PAYS THE BILLS WHILE MAKING ROOM IN YOUR LIFE FOR THE THINGS YOU'RE MOST ENTHUSIASTIC ABOUT.

We know scientifically that our thinking has a direct impact on the cells in our bodies. This means that doing something we don't feel inspired or called to do affects our overall mental health and physical well-being. Think about how much influence those eight hours or more you spend working most days have on everything else, from your quality of sleep and energy levels to how many resources (time, money, energy) you have available to pursue your passions. There is no doubt your work has an impact on your sense of vitality. When your work isn't working, it can create a snowball effect in which even your rest time, including time with family and friends or hobbies that previously felt joyful, no longer fills your spirit. That kind of negative feedback loop can be tough to break, and an unhappy work situation can go from bad to ugly in a hurry.

Now think about the ripple effects felt throughout your entire organization if there's no sense of fulfillment in the very work you're doing to begin with. How can any member of your team possibly hope to find satisfaction in their work if they don't have a strong and purposeful foundation to lift them up? The good news is that we can leverage that snowball effect for good. Encouraging your team to find meaning in their work leads to a sense of purpose that can go beyond feeling motivated to complete the day's required tasks. Being fulfilled at work will seep into the rest of life just as much as being unfulfilled at work will, creating a positive feedback loop instead of a negative one.

I happen to work in a role that allows me to interact with ministers and clergy from many faith traditions. Often in coffeehouse chats, we have discussed the life of service, which frequently includes a reference to a "calling," a deep knowing within of what needs to be done, which path to take. While not all of us want to be ministers or even work in spiritual spaces, I'd like you to consider that we all have a deep calling from within. And I think it is important to honor that calling. That doesn't mean we won't have tough days, but when we do, the bigger picture of honoring our calling will move us through those days with much less resistance and suffering.

There's the old saying that when you do what you love, you never work a day in your life. When we are able to find and live out our true callings, we enjoy every minute of it. We take great pleasure in the work we do and have a sense of satisfaction and joy. Think about the best roles you've ever held. I bet they honored, at least in some small way, your true calling. Even when things got tough or there were bad days (and there always are), a purposeful position offers an opportunity to find passion, gratitude, and fun. Life is short. Every one of us deserves to do what we truly love. When we are doing what feeds our spirit, we will arise each day with enthusiasm and optimism and be our most successful and joyful selves.

It is also important to note that your calling may not be your paying job. Throughout the years, I have seen a movement toward celebrating the call to "do what you love" and "honor your calling." These maxims can be uplifting, inspirational, and even life-changing. They can and do create a ripple effect throughout our experience, drawing us to greater purpose. However, it is essential to recognize that many people may not be able to make a living doing what they love.

Many people may not even *want* to turn their passions into their careers. Sometimes when we turn what we love doing into a means of income, we lose some of the joy that drew us to that field, activity, or skill in the first place. As a result, it's easy to feel pressured to realign our priorities or make drastic changes in our work. It can even feel like failure when we're unable to both do what we love *and* make a living at it. But that's a false sense of failure.

It is possible, and sometimes actually preferable, to have a job that allows you to pay the bills while also making room in your life for the things you're most enthusiastic about. When you find yourself on such a path—or actively choose it for yourself—you still get to create the same positive ripple effect in your life. The key here is to honor your calling no matter what, even if you have other means of supporting yourself and your family financially. Remembering this when we say "do what you love" can help remove the guilt, shame, or pressure we might otherwise feel from these well-intentioned life messages.

For instance, I love my yoga practice. It brings me great peace and is super healthy for me. Since I was introduced to it more than a decade ago, my mat and my practice call to me just as being hungry does when I need to eat. It has become a foundational pillar of my existence. There was a time early on when I loved my yoga so much that I thought about becoming an instructor and doing it all the time. But as a young parent then with school-age children, it was simply not a practical means for me to contribute financially to our family at the level we needed. I chose instead to make time to do the yoga I loved in the form of classes, retreats, and even yoga trips, while choosing a more financially stable path to sustain our family. Similarly, I have friends who love to garden but don't necessarily want to open a nursery, or who relax by cooking an elaborate meal but would never choose to open a restaurant. Doing something we love doesn't mean we have to make a living at it. It just means we need to make time for it as a part of our commitment to healthy, balanced self-care.

When we honor our calling in whatever form, we will find that we more naturally live in the flow of life. We seem to be always in the right place at the right time, with the right people and solutions showing up to help us along the way. We allow and are more tolerant of change and things that happen in our lives, rather than being in a constant state of resistance. Passion is awakened when you feel connected, bringing energy

SPIRITUAL ACTIVITIES CAN BE ANYTHING THAT WE DO WITH A SPIRIT CONSCIOUSNESS, WITH A SENSE OF LOVE, SERVICE, OR KINDNESS.

and verve to even the most mundane aspects of your work. That passion is the fuel to achieving your most extraordinary life, and it's ignited when you are in alignment with what you have been called to do. Doing what we have always wanted to do creates focus, like sunlight through a magnifying glass, allowing you to avoid distraction. This is how you can build a life with a feeling of satisfaction, how you can nurture an overall sense of peace and well-being. This is how you fulfill your sense of spiritual connection.

The truth is that any job, task, or activity can be made spiritual. In almost everything we do, there is power in *how* we do it. We often think about the things we do as having an inherent nature of their own, separate from how we ourselves approach it. Spiritual activities, then, aren't just attending a service or engaging in prayer or studying a religious text. They can be anything that we do with a spirit consciousness, with a sense of love, service, or kindness. The *spiritual* part comes from us.

This is a practice I'm working on with myself, bringing this evolution in ideology into my own life. I'm learning that my own deepest inner calling is to be of service. This resonates with me as I start to look at everything through this new lens. Within the confines of any task on any day, I can honor my calling by approaching it with the intention to be of service. In my daily work routine, I can prioritize actively listening to a coworker, holding doors open for others, offering to get someone a drink, or pick up lunch. In these small but important ways, I have the opportunity to support myself and my family with my job while honoring my calling to serve each and every day. Another example is to take my professional and intellectual gifts and apply them at an organization that has a powerful mission or is doing some form of good in the world. Reframing how I think about these activities proves my capacity for making a living at the same time I honor my calling to make a difference in the world through service.

Now imagine that every person on your team benefits from that central purpose in their work. Everyone feels committed to the higher aims, fulfilling a broader goal. That is the power of a mission statement. When an organization does the work to define its *why* and can integrate that with the mission, it is naturally aligned with its organizational calling in the world. And now you have something to measure your success against. Rather than ending up in a position of drifting in one direction or another, or only vaguely heading toward a generic goal, you have a purpose that informs your strategy.

It's been said that what can be measured can be managed. Knowing where you want to end up—whatever your organization's mission—is the most surefire way to set your team up for success. You can't generate a blueprint if you don't already have the end result in mind. Getting that part ironed out can make identifying key milestones, pinpointing potential gaps or problem areas, and defining team-level objectives (as well as individual goals) go much more smoothly.

WHEN AN ORGANIZATION DEFINES ITS *WHY* AND CAN INTEGRATE IT WITH THE MISSION, IT ALIGNS WITH ITS ORGANIZATIONAL CALLING IN THE WORLD.

If you have associates, teams, or departments that are all too happy to go with the flow, performing tasks as needed without any sort of metrics or measurements for success, it can be difficult to spot when things aren't going as planned. That's why a clear mission is also an essential process for determining how to know when you're *not* on track. Maybe at a glance you see the bottom line or other primary metric is improving, but you don't realize things are falling apart in another area. Failing to keep your overarching mission at the forefront of your planning and review processes can mean you're leaving key components of your organizational success to chance.

Collective Creativity and Consciousness

Though they may seem largely unrelated at first glance, business best practices and spiritual principles can, in fact, intersect and even support each other. While they may not always have the same ends in mind, the truth is that they're both ways to help us reach our potential and flourish within our environment.

The first area where we often see that business and spiritual practices can align for organizational success is the installation of a mission or purpose statement.

The latest guidance in the business world is that a mission statement needs to be short, compelling, and memorable. There's not much use in a mission statement that your team doesn't know, but that's exactly what often happens. Some surveys have shown that fewer than half of employees are able to repeat their organization's mission statement. This is frequently the result of a statement that is disconnected from the culture or the work being accomplished, or one that lacks any real meaning for the associates serving in the organization. Or it may simply be that the statement is too long or unwieldy, making it difficult to remember.

Maybe you're not convinced that a mission or values statement is particularly important to your organization's success. Many organizations also have employee handbooks or bylaws or other guiding documentation that are only referenced when necessary. You might be thinking that doing the work to create a short, compelling, and memorable mission statement is unnecessary or even a waste of time. But having an engaging mission statement is vitally important to organizational success for two main reasons. The first is that a compelling mission statement helps spark a collective creative process for the entire culture. It becomes the foundational idea that, when supported by the appropriate words and actions, can lead the organization to achieving its goals and meeting its ultimate, successful outcome. A mission statement establishes in the group's consciousness what they are trying to do and, as such, is a perfect example of how New Thought principles and business best practices overlap.

In New Thought teachings, we know that our thoughts and feelings create our experience of life, which is why the notion of holding a collective consciousness around a specific idea is such a profound concept. This is where the power of affirmative thought really shines. We have the capacity to manifest the outcomes we seek in life, becoming cocreators for the highest good. This is possible because we attract like energy with our thoughts and intentions, drawing more of what we seek to us through visualization and affirmation. The more people focus together on an idea or outcome, the more energy and action are transferred in the direction of that idea—which increases the probability of manifestation.

Have you ever noticed how long it takes (and how much energy it requires) to order lunch for a group of people when each person has their own ideas about what constitutes a good lunch—the type of food, the quality of service, the speed of delivery? How does that change when you start out with a specific restaurant in mind? At least now you're all going in the same direction. That still doesn't mean everyone orders the same meal, but you have narrowed the focus. Likewise, when multiple individuals in an organization are inspired by the mission statement and are carrying the same thoughts toward the end goal, then universal spiritual principles, the science of energy transfer, and even the theories of quantum physics are all now aligned in their favor.

The second reason for having a mission statement that is thoughtful, short, and compelling is that it will be more useful—and more meaningful—to individuals and teams within the organization. Even a perfectly aligned mission statement that is two pages long won't be of much practical use—there's just too much to digest. Here are a few examples of short, memorable, and compelling mission statements that are centered in the purpose of the organization:

- JetBlue: "To inspire humanity—both in the air and on the ground."
- Tesla: "To accelerate the world's transition to sustainable energy."
- TED: "Spread ideas."
- LinkedIn: "Connect the world's professionals to make them more productive and successful."

There is a place for longer-form exploration of your organizational goals, but when it comes to defining the core mission, short and sweet is the ticket. The bigger your organization, the more important this is. Think of the companies on the Fortune 500 list: They are, of course, made up of a variety of departments and teams ranging from finance and accounting to marketing and sales, not to mention research and development, legal, customer service, and just about anything in between.

Working for a corporate giant on their social media team will be a vastly different experience than serving on their board of directors, but the people serving in both roles must have the same ultimate mission in mind at the end of the day. When people can easily remember and refer to it, the mission statement becomes the compass or touchstone for guiding all decision-making and strategy at every level of the org chart. It can operate as a lead principle for all behavior in an organization. It becomes a living, breathing group affirmation toward an organization's intended consequence.

As an example of the power of a short and inspiring mission statement, a survey of more than 300 employees where I work at Unity Village revealed 79 percent of the workforce could recall all or part of the mission statement: "To help and serve more people through prayer, publishing, and community." That number is significantly higher than many other surveys asking how many employees can recite their company's mission statement. The development of a compelling mission statement is a corporate best practice. From a spiritual perspective, it can be an affirmation of who you are and want to be in the world, serving as the foundation of your collective creative process.

Aligning Your Values

Value statements, much like a mission statement, are a guiding set of principles for how an organization engages both with those it serves and with each other. Value statements, again when they have been written to be short and compelling, can serve as a compass for preferred behavior inside the organization. They act as a reminder for what is most important to the organization and the skills and attributes most essential to the overall mission.

To make value statements even more effective, organizations can build them into their performance review systems with a section dedicated to how well the employees exhibit and model the organization's core values. This simple practice provides a boundary that is often absent in organizational culture. It is very easy to say, "Well, we expect everyone to do their jobs well and to treat each other with respect." But how does that usually end up playing out in the day-to-day life of an organization? "Oh, that's just how Bob is. He is cranky and hard to deal with, but he is good at his job."

When core values are included in the performance management system, the organization does not have to tolerate a toxic personality simply because someone does good work. Organizations—and all committed associates, congregants, or members who do observe and model the value system—deserve to have people serving in and among them who are both good at their jobs *and* good citizens of the organization's culture. When values are applied this way, they become an affirmation for what is (and is not) acceptable in a culture. This also works as a practical barometer for measuring value alignment and for preserving a healthy and enlightened culture in which people are respectful and accountable to one another.

In spiritual circles, it is a common practice to set intentions. When people gather together—whether for worship, a retreat, a class, a meeting, or a book study—the leader often opens with an intention or establishes a container that sets forth an agreement for shared values for the group's time together. Values at an organizational level can work the same way, whether or not you frame them as intentions or affirmations. They are a deeply centered agreement among those who are serving that the established values will guide their time or service together.

In exploring how a cohesive mission and values work within an organization, it might be helpful to understand the creative process as it is taught in New Thought circles. In its simplest form, the creative process is the evolution of thoughts or ideas as they are transformed into affirmative, spoken words and then supported by appropriate actions. This is how we align thought, word, and action as a collective group. When we're struggling to manifest a desired outcome—particularly when working within an organization—

THE CREATIVE PROCESS IS THE EVOLUTION OF THOUGHTS OR IDEAS TRANSFORMED INTO SPOKEN WORDS THEN SUPPORTED BY APPROPRIATE ACTIONS.

it's commonly because we're making an error by not ensuring that all three elements are truly aligned. For instance, I may take an idea I want to manifest and create affirmations and spoken words to support it, but then either I don't take any action or my actions don't align with the consciousness I am trying to establish.

Here's a personal example: There have been times in my life when I wanted to be more physically fit. I would begin by thinking positive thoughts about my body and choosing affirmations like *I am lean* or *I am strong*. Looking back, however, I can see that my actions were not in alignment with my words. I neglected to adjust my diet properly to support these affirmations, and my exercise programs were inconsistent at best.

Organizationally, I have seen teams that desire to be more prosperous. They hold a vision in mind and they say the right words, but all of their actions and activity are focused on cutting costs. Being mindful of spending is not bad, obviously, and certainly is a part of good stewardship, but cutting costs cannot lead you to prosperity.

There must be activity focused toward generating greater revenue and income—new ideas, new products, anything that creates space for greater prosperity. Choose to develop consciousness around creating something more, rather than making something less. The creative process relies upon having all three elements—thoughts, words, and actions—in alignment, or you will suffer an inconsistent result. And as in these examples, the most common way misalignment shows up is usually in the action element.

Considering this now in the larger context, it can be all too easy to simply declare success once we feel we've gotten the words right, finalizing the language of our mission and values but not extending their meaning to our actions. If your organization deems accessibility a core value of your operations, but you don't implement usability standards on your website or alter your building's entrances to accommodate all visitors or provide closed captioning for your audio content, your values still aren't reflected in your organization. Your mission hasn't extended beyond documentation. This can be a particularly easy mistake to make in spiritually based organizations. We place such an emphasis on prayer, meditation, and affirmative thinking—which are all essential to improving our overall consciousness—that we overlook the final step: action. It is certainly true that managing our thoughts can change our lives, but we must remember that it's not managing our thoughts *alone* that makes change possible. Within Unity teachings, this is our fifth principle, which is loosely stated as, "We must live the truth we know." That means taking right action alongside practicing right thought.

When I first came to Unity, the organizational culture was not particularly healthy. There were many issues, including a severe disconnect between the associates and the leadership. A lack of trust and transparency led to many in the organization focusing primarily on all the things that were perceived to be wrong and a reluctance to see solutions or opportunities to repair a sense of connection. This manifested as lots of negativity and a near-constant hum of complaints. This was disheartening for me, particularly because the work we do at Unity is transformative for so many people's lives. There were—and still are—an abundance of testimonials each week about how this organization helps people in their times of need. Even so, all of the attention internally was focused on what was lacking. It was not a positive or uplifting environment.

With the help of our People Support team, I began a campus-wide campaign called *#MyWhy*. We printed up small cards, about the size of an index card, with some of the most iconic images of Unity Village and blank lines for each associate to fill out. We then asked every associate to contemplate their "why" for serving at Unity and write it on their chosen card. We displayed those cards on plexiglass boards in different places around campus, rotating the card displays twice a year. We also asked each associate to keep a copy of their card at their desk as a touchstone reminder of their reason for being here, especially when they had a particularly challenging day or experience. It helped them recall the bigger picture of why they were at Unity and the good work the organization was doing.

Still today, you can find these boards on campus with our associates' own "why" for working at Unity. They are a constant reminder to all who traverse the halls of our buildings of why we do what we do. Here is a sampling from the associates:

- To make a difference in people's lives. To meet them where they are with no judgment but with compassion and love. To go on this journey together.
- It's all about the people and the purpose. I come to campus and spend my workdays with friends, not merely coworkers, but real friends. People to laugh with, cry with, try with. And we are here working together. Reaching out to people, striving to make their days better. Endeavoring to make the world a better place through positivity and inspiration and prayer … every day.
- I serve because I want to make a difference in the world. It's not just about money; it's about making our world a better place to live!

This simple campaign was the beginning of a huge transition in our culture. Slowly but surely, the focus began to shift to the positive aspects of their individual contributions as well as the overall mission and impact that Unity has all over the world. This change in perspective had a tremendous impact on our team, and it also provided the leadership team with a huge repository of anecdotal data that helped us guide the definition of our mission and values. Through the study of the individual *#MyWhy* cards, the values and most important facets of our associates' and leadership team's experience could easily be seen—and the broader themes and commonalities rose to the top. These themes were then used to help define the new mission and values.

Avoiding Common Missteps

Unfortunately, anything as important as your organization's mission statement will also be at risk for missteps or pitfalls. The important thing is to be aware of how crafting a meaningful mission statement can go wrong and to be ready to pivot when it does.

The first thing is to be mindful that a mission statement belongs to the entirety of the organization. It's not the executive team's or just for the managers or just for your highest-revenue department. It is for everyone! As an organization's leader, it can be particularly easy to feel our own passion and purpose get wrapped up in our organization's mission. One of the signs of a successful leader is, after all, a deep connection with the organization's goals. But no matter how closely your personal values align with the company's, you must remember that the mission statement belongs to all. That means being able to separate yourself by a degree and to welcome additional perspectives.

Just as it's unwise to attempt branding an organization with a mission that doesn't reflect the company culture or existing values, it's also important to seek a wide variety of perspectives. While you may be able to get substantial feedback from each member of your team if your organization is small enough, most larger organizations simply cannot request input from every person to help find your *why* and define a mission. That said, you can (and should) collect and reference data with demographic reports, team surveys, feedback forms, and more throughout the mission-building process. Gather both anecdotal and quantifiable data from associates early on to learn about their perceptions of the organization, how they would define your values, and what they see for the future. This is invaluable information for helping you define a mission that connects with those serving the organization—and helps create an engaging dialogue as you prepare various iterations for review. You don't have to incorporate every piece of feedback you get, of course. But ideally, by the time you unveil your final mission statement and values, no one should be surprised. They should already relate to the core of your *why*.

Great leadership doesn't happen from the top down, and neither should your mission statement. As you have conversations about the heart of your organization and

ANOTHER EASY SNAG TO HIT IS FOCUSING ON ASPIRATIONAL VALUES OR CRAFTING A MISSION STATEMENT FOR AN IDEALIZED VERSION OF YOUR ORGANIZATION.

how to move it forward, ask yourself who is not sitting at the table. Unlike many executive functions—forecasting the future, performing risk analysis, allocating resources—a mission statement can't (and shouldn't) be enforced by those in a position of authority. You'll need to open up the conversation to anyone who has a stake in your organization's success. Ask those serving with you for honest feedback, ensuring that your mission and values are defined from the ground up. It will also help ensure that the language resonates throughout the organization because they were part of its creation. It gives the team a sense of ownership over the mission, which will also help people remember it and be willing to affirm it.

Be careful, though! If you focus so much on wordsmithing your statement, you might lose sight of the intended meaning behind those words. I am a big believer in thoughtful contemplation and meditation. When working on something of particular importance—or anytime I feel stuck—I sleep on it. During my time away from actively engaging with it, I go into the Silence and ask the wisdom of my heart for clarity. The Silence is an important meditative tool in Unity, a still and quiet place for expressing affirmative thoughts or prayers and for engaging with Spirit. The act of stepping away and letting go creates a space for innovation and creativity to emerge, allowing thoughts or ideas to come to the surface that wouldn't have shown up during phases of active work.

Another way to approach this process is with the agile methodology, which has become a popular tool in industries from application development to marketing. The agile framework is good for any type of creative endeavor, relying on shorter stages or iterations of effort and promoting quick response to change instead of following a plan without deviation. As you have no doubt experienced yourself, the scope and timelines for large projects are constantly changing; the agile method cuts through all that by focusing on incremental progress rather than getting bogged down in the plan for the project in its entirety. This ensures that each revision is timely and more relevant to the current needs of the project and prevents excessive shifting of the overall scope and timeline. By considering your efforts to define a mission statement as iterations or passes, it can take the pressure off and allow creativity and innovation to flow naturally. We don't always get it right the first time, and that is okay! Acknowledging that up front can help us change our psychology, allowing us to see things as a first (or second or third or …) draft on our way to getting to the heart of our mission.

Another easy snag to hit is focusing on aspirational values or crafting a mission statement that is designed to fit an idealized version of your organization. When you ignore the reality of your organization's current culture, you're likely to confuse your people and fall short of your vision. And in the end, no one is going to feel a tangible connection with the heart of the mission.

The trick is to figure out what is already important to your people, what is already promoted by your culture, and polish those values to the best version of themselves. If your organization today prioritizes an exceptional customer service experience, suddenly defining your values around innovation and taking risks on new ideas is likely to cause some major conflict. But if your mission helps deepen the connection to customer service, embracing the value of great service and encouraging an outstanding experience all around, people will buy in emotionally because you're speaking to what they already believe in.

Gems from Part Two: Mission Critical

- Identify *why* your organization does what it does before you begin to create a mission statement. What is the purpose, cause, or belief that drives it?
- Too many people work in unfulfilling jobs that take a toll on their physical and mental well-being. Lead your team to find meaning or a central purpose in their work.
- Discern your true calling. What feeds your spirit? It may or may not be your paying job. If not, do what you love on the side.
- Any job, task, or activity can be made spiritual because spirituality is in us. Approach any job with a sense of love, service, or kindness.
- Keep your mission statement short, compelling, and memorable. It establishes the group's consciousness and focuses everyone on a specific idea or outcome, which increases the probability of manifestation.

- Value statements are a guiding set of principles for how people in an organization treat each other and those they serve. You are setting intentions that will guide your service together.

- Make values a part of performance reviews. They are skills and attributes essential to the overall mission. Don't tolerate toxic behavior, even from someone who does a good job.

- Thoughts, words, and actions must be aligned. Simply speaking words or posting a mission statement on the wall is not enough. Intentions must be implemented.

- A mission statement is not top-down. Seek a wide variety of perspectives. It gives the team a sense of ownership in the mission.

- Work in short bursts. You might go through many drafts of a mission statement.

- Align the mission and value statements with your organization's current culture and what is important to them, not an idealized version.

PART THREE

Enlightening the Leaders

Developing a Leadership Philosophy

Once you have a mission and values established—and your people have bought into them—it's time to figure out how to lead in bringing the mission and values to life. Just as the first step you take on a journey can't also be your last, you will need to create ongoing momentum and support through active leadership.

As important as establishing a consistent leadership philosophy is to the success of an organization, it is an often-overlooked step. When you neglect to build consistent leadership, the culture never fully develops into a cohesive ecosystem as intended because there is a hodgepodge of incompatible and inconsistent leadership philosophies at play. If developing a mission statement is like creating a blueprint for organizational success, creating consistent leadership is like having a good contractor. You need someone (or a team of people) to help coordinate all the moving pieces and to provide guidance for bringing it all together to support the common goal.

Discordant or dysfunctional leadership practices can result in an inconsistent experience of the organization and its culture for each associate, depending on who their leaders are. It can also create headaches when identifying key performance indicators and trying to reach organizational goals. Everyone might agree on where you're going, but no one is on the same page about how to get there. By requiring every leader to adopt the same leadership philosophy, organizations become consistent in the values, practices, and tenets of leadership. Every associate can expect and experience consistency from any leader, no matter what role they hold.

It also serves to solidify commonality at the leadership level, so everyone is moving forward in the same direction. That doesn't mean that each department, team, or associate works in exactly the same way. Instead, it helps ensure that there are no surprises when someone is promoted and has a different supervisor or manager. Like having a mission statement that an entire organization feels committed to, having a consistent leadership philosophy provides a common set of values to work from. This framework helps develop an overall sense of trust and frees up mental bandwidth to tackle other projects or problems.

How do you choose a common leadership philosophy, and how do you implement it across an organization? First, let's look at some common philosophies that should be avoided. They might get results in the short-term, which is often tempting when you're in the midst of a project or feel pressure to make something happen quickly. The drawback is that they can create even bigger problems in the long term.

BY REQUIRING EVERY LEADER TO ADOPT THE SAME LEADERSHIP PHILOSOPHY, ORGANIZATIONS BECOME CONSISTENT IN THE VALUES, PRACTICES, AND TENETS OF LEADERSHIP.

Leadership through fear or intimidation can inspire quick bursts of productivity and the capacity to meet deadlines or important milestones but at the cost of your associates' own sense of value or well-being. That can rapidly create high turnover rates, a sense of toxicity across whole teams or departments, and the impression that escalating intimidation is needed to continue to get things done. In environments that rely on fear and intimidation, employees are so focused on not making errors that any room for creativity—or even enjoyment—is squeezed out.

Even less obviously toxic tactics can lead to problems. With a command-and-control hierarchy, for instance, you typically have just one person who holds authority and controls the decision-making power. The authoritarian leader provides the command, and the control portion comes in the form of curtailing any behavior in the lower ranks that doesn't involve performing tasks as instructed. There is little room for input, innovation, or individual creativity in command-and-control leadership environments. There are clear requirements and standards that must be met in each facet of your organization. That may seem attractive when you're trying to establish consistency, but in the long run it can create feelings of disempowerment and distrust.

Likewise, in top-down leadership situations, all goals and objectives are determined by the executives and filtered down through subsequent levels of management. There is little incentive for innovation, creativity, or improvement at the ground floor. These leadership styles can lead not only to burnout and resentment throughout your organization, but they can also mean missed opportunities. You have closed off avenues to getting input and ideas from those who are closest to the work.

Finding a Better Way

I have served under both a command-and-control leadership philosophy and one that was driven by fear and intimidation. My experience in both settings was very negative. Each had such a profound impact on me, both personally and professionally, that I knew if I ever had the chance to help develop a culture myself, neither style would be tolerated. I knew there had to be a better way.

The command-and-control leadership environment came early in my career at a large financial institution. Our division leader was a seasoned executive who was not to be challenged—ever. Doing so, either publicly or privately, would ultimately lead to a person's separating from the organization, sometimes by their own choice and sometimes by his. His authoritative nature definitely got things done. Unfortunately, this led to hundreds of

EVEN MINOR TRANSGRESSIONS LIKE A MISSED DEADLINE ON A MEANINGLESS TASK WOULD LEAD TO HARSH OR SNARKY COMMENTS ABOUT HOW WORTHLESS WE WERE.

missed opportunities for improvement to our overall operations. No one below him could provide suggestions or ideas for improvement, even though the solutions were obvious to those doing the work. Most command-and-control environments are filled with aged systems, outdated processes, and a deeply uninspired workforce. That was certainly my experience, at least.

I have also served in roles in which, though not obvious at the outset, the leaders I reported to thrived on leading by fear and intimidation. In organizations that rely on this leadership style, leaders use their title and higher-ranking position to pressure employees. Those employees end up constantly stressed, afraid, or intimidated. They aren't focused on doing better but on not making a mistake. As you can imagine, this is very damaging and demoralizing to all. It also ends up impacting employees' personal lives as the pressure and constant fear of losing their jobs are nearly impossible to leave at the office.

In one instance, I had a leader whose practice included dressing down those on our team, seemingly every day. I worked in IT, so there were the occasional system outages that would impact other employees and business productivity as a whole. During those outage times, which are already pressure-packed and anxiety-ridden, this gentleman would stand right over our shoulders. He would often shout about how and why we had not done something to prevent this problem. This would be followed by more insults and shouting about how long it was taking to fix the problem. You can imagine what it was like trying to diagnose complex problems in technical systems with a person berating you through the entire experience. After the incident was resolved, we would once again be told that if we didn't figure out how to prevent this from ever happening again, we would be replaced. Even minor transgressions like a missed deadline on a meaningless task would lead to harsh or snarky comments about how worthless we were.

I was not long for that role. This leadership style is, by far, the unhealthiest for anyone serving under them. We know the impact of stress and fear on our physical and emotional bodies can be pronounced and can have serious short- and long-term consequences. From disruptions in appetite and sleep to headaches, nausea, fatigue, and increased blood pressure—it's not something to take lightly. I experienced some of these side effects, including physical symptoms and a toll on my personal relationships. It is because of my experience in these two styles that I consider them intolerable when establishing a healthy, thriving culture.

Adopting Servant Leadership

Luckily, a shift is occurring. In for-profit and spiritual organizations alike, a new leadership paradigm has emerged over the past decade or two known as servant leadership—another perfect example of where we can allow spiritual principles and business best practices to overlap. Unlike some of the other styles we've discussed here, this leadership philosophy embodies many of the same values and principles you would expect in a spiritually inclined, enlightened, nonprofit organization. In a nutshell, servant leadership reverses the old top-down paradigm of CEOs, directors, and managers being supported by the rest of the associates. Instead, those serving in the day-to-day, task-oriented roles are at the top of the pyramid, supported by the leadership teams. A servant leader's job is to be of service to those task-oriented roles by removing obstacles that prevent their success, making sure they have the necessary resources to function at the highest level, and providing compassionate leadership and development to help them grow as people. With this as the goal, it is easy to see that the servant leadership philosophy embodies the intersection of spiritual principle and business best practices.

Robert K. Greenleaf, the founder of the modern servant leadership movement and the Greenleaf Center for Servant Leadership, defines it this way on his website: "Servant leadership is a philosophy and set of practices that enriches the lives of individuals, builds better organizations, and ultimately creates a more just and caring world." He outlines the principles of servant leadership: listening, healing, empathy, awareness, persuasion, conceptualization, foresight, stewardship, commitment to growth, and building community. Compare these to the foundations of top-down or command-and-control leadership and consider how different the experiences are likely to be for your associates. With servant leadership, you have an opportunity to develop an engaging conversation rather than becoming a taskmaster. You have an opportunity to create something bigger than yourself, which is typically what led us to leadership work in the first place.

This is also the most direct way to ensure that your diverse workforce feels supported and appreciated. In positions of leadership, especially early on in a new role, we are often encouraged to step into another's shoes to better understand the range of perspectives and experiences of our teams and our community. And there's good reason for that exercise in empathy. As a servant leader, you are committed to hearing from a whole chorus of voices rather than just your own. When you change the focus from how *you* think the organization should operate to how the operators themselves can best succeed, you have immediately opened your mind to a wider range of perspectives and needs. This means being able to hear different lived experiences, new perceptions, and other opinions about organizational success.

A more practical and approachable description of servant leadership may be found in a blog post from S. Vasudev, a principal consultant at PM Power Consulting, who defines the seven pillars of servant leadership as follows: person of character, puts people first, skilled communicator, compassionate collaborator, has foresight, systems thinker, and leads with moral authority. Those same characteristics would be sought for any spiritual leadership role as well.

When I returned to Unity as CEO, there was a mix of styles at play. While there were some command-and-control and fear-and-intimidation practices in use, there were also a few leaders who did not realize they were modeling the principles of servant leadership. What I had come to notice at Unity, and in some of my other roles at large organizations, is that a person's lived experience of company culture could be very different based on the leadership style in play in their area. When we were first turning the tide toward a healthier culture at Unity, we would hear rave reviews from associates with testaments of gratitude. Then we would find pockets of people who, despite seeing some things change, were still unhappy and unfulfilled. After diagnosing about three of these areas, I could see they

FOR EVERYONE TO ENJOY THE BENEFITS OF A HEALTHY CULTURE, EVERY LEADER NEEDS TO BE LEADING FROM THE SAME PLAYBOOK.

all had one thing in common: a leadership style that did not match the culture we were creating.

That's when it became clear to our vice president of People Support and me that for *everyone* to enjoy the benefits of a healthy culture, every leader needed to be leading from the same playbook. Though an individual's style of servant leadership may vary a little, differing because of their personality or background, they still need to model the primary tenets of being of service to the members of their teams. This will ensure that the lived experience of our associates is one of inclusiveness, support, and appreciation—even across different departments and teams.

No matter how cohesive your organizational leadership style is, it's still important to honor the diversity in behavioral styles. Servant leadership will look a little different depending on each leader's personality, background, and work style.

Leading with a New Perspective

When I first returned to lead Unity, I had a voluminous appetite for new ideas and projects. I would bring several to each meeting with our executive team. I was working to create as much positive change as quickly as possible. After the first few weeks, I began to experience what I thought was opposition to many of these ideas and endeavors. I began to privately get frustrated with how resistant to change some of the team seemed to be and with how long it was taking us to make decisions and move forward. This pattern continued for the first few months and seemed to be a big obstacle for me.

Then a moment of serendipity occurred. One of the new initiatives I brought forth was for our executive and leadership team to attend a multiday session on behavioral styles. This was similar to a Myers-Briggs Type Indicator exercise—a way to inventory worldview and decision-making preferences. I liked this particular solution because it references an individual's behavior style rather than their personality. Offered by the Effectiveness Institute, it assesses individual behavioral styles both in the workplace and at home. It doesn't define the person but rather identifies and quantifies their preferred way of operating.

Lo and behold, what I was experiencing with my team was not resistance at all. Their styles just required something different. My particular style relies on quick decisions, broad vision, high-level strategies, and the ability to "see around the corner." Their styles required more data, more details, or, in some cases, just more time to consider or talk about what was being presented.

With this new perspective, I began to modify how I presented new ideas and initiatives. I began to use much more data and far more detail. I started providing more time to consider each one. I would present the information in one meeting, and we would discuss it again at a later meeting. This brought about a miraculous change in our sense of efficiency, communication, and teamwork. Everyone felt seen, heard, and respected for their individual behavioral styles and the gifts they brought to the table. We stopped operating in a one-size-fits-all approach. Even today we rely on each other in that way by celebrating our unique styles.

There is a valuable lesson here for leaders. We must be aware of the differences in styles and, at the same time, be willing to adjust our behaviors in an effort to honor the specific needs of other styles. We need to meet people where they are. The more we can consider the differences in how people hear and process information—the more we are willing to listen intently to what is being said and not said, rather than jumping to conclusions—the more effective we will be in our communications, relationships, and service.

Here are my own tenets of servant leadership, the ones that I strive to incorporate every day in my work as a CEO and a leader of people:

Tenet 1: Prioritize People

Your people are your engine. You won't get anywhere without your associates or the members of your organization. Their wellness, growth, and success should be prioritized above all else. Yes, systems and processes and best practices will help your organization run better and more efficiently, but you can't "efficiency" your way out of a toxic workplace or an environment of mistrust.

Tenet 2: Create Transparency

Trust is a two-way street. Just as actively listening to your associates creates a healthy working relationship, so does being honest and open with what you have to share. This makes some leaders nervous, but it shouldn't. Creating transparency does not mean total openness in all matters, but it does mean a willingness to share your own plans for the future, to nurture a sense of collective buy-in, and to acknowledge issues or mistakes.

Tenet 3: Focus on the Future

Servant leaders must keep one eye on what's coming up next—in six months, in five years, in 20 years. When you're in the business of building something that lasts, you can't let your focus on the future drift. This process is, by its very nature, an evolution. You must be willing to adjust, recalibrate, and keep moving forward. Without this focus forward, your organization or ministry may lose relevancy in the long term. Innovation and modernization help you stay in step with social and technological evolutions while still serving your customers or community.

REMIND YOUR
TEAM THAT IF
THIS DOESN'T
WORK, WE'LL
TRY SOMETHING
ELSE!

Tenet 4: Compassion in All Things

One key component missing from many hierarchical leadership styles is something that we, as human beings, absolutely need to thrive: compassion. A little can go a very long way. One of the ways compassion can show up in the workplace is operating from a place of being willing to put yourself in another's shoes. To be supportive when there are family or personal issues. To be sensitive to life events that associates are experiencing. It can also be in the form of creating room for people to make mistakes without punitive repercussions while still challenging and encouraging them to be better. Be compassionate by listening to those you serve with, be present with them and whatever they are struggling with regardless of how you may view their circumstance. Be unwilling to sacrifice this point in order to save time or cut corners. It will help you deepen your relationship with your associates, with your organization, and with your broader community or industry.

While introducing a new leadership approach can take some getting used to for individual team members, it can also create some tension with an organization's heritage. Shifting an organization's culture from its historical posture is not easy, and it certainly takes time. Patience and perseverance are both important to be successful. As leaders, it is important not to resent the past or previous leaders' styles or decisions. Instead, focus on what you can do well now and how your approach will create positive change. This will lift you out of the mentality of focusing on what you are against and free you to focus time, energy, and effort on what you are striving to promote.

Many will carry with them the failed initiatives of the past—failed efforts in some of the same areas you are trying to improve—and it can lead to a lot of "but we already tried that" rhetoric and attitudes. A good approach to this obstacle is acknowledging those past attempts or missteps while sharing why you want to try it again and, importantly, why you think it will be successful *this* time. Things change, and sometimes it's simply a matter of bad timing. People (particularly in companies, congregations, or organizations with long legacies) often fear change because what has been done in the past did work—at least to some extent. They're still there, after all.

Surviving, of course, is not the same as thriving, and we must learn to accept change in order to grow. Emphasize your commitment to creating positive change, not simply to whatever specific approach or change you have proposed. Remind your team that if this doesn't work, we'll try something else! This allows people to release the feelings of permanence related to forthcoming changes and to embrace the possibility that it's an experiment that may just work. The key is always to respectfully acknowledge the leaders and past initiatives while remaining firm and affirmative in the new direction.

Choosing How You Show Up

Just as we saw with the development of a mission statement, crafting that vision and honing that language is only the first step. Without relevant and meaningful action, a leadership philosophy is just words on a page. Defining how you want leadership to look in your organization is a crucial foundational element, but it will ultimately be meaningless unless you work to create that vision. That can show up a couple of different ways in your work, both on the macro level (through standard operating procedures and communication cadences and annual review processes) and on the micro level (in how you and your organization's leaders show up every day).

This leadership philosophy really hinges on a thought practice, and that is important because it creates a foundation for everything else that we work with. Some might consider this a provocative concept, but the truth is that every single day, you have the power to choose your experience. Being a strong leader when it's time to forecast for the year ahead or empower your associates through a difficult season is admirable. But it's just as important to evoke your servant leadership philosophy on any given Tuesday.

I know, I know, I can hear the myriad responses now: "Jim, I don't choose the weather, the rude people, the malfunctioning computers, appliances, automobiles, and so on. Nor do I choose the serious events in life that happen to me, my family, or my friends." I get it, and I am not suggesting that we are somehow in control of every event that may occur during the course of our lifetimes—or the wide array of challenges and hiccups that our organizations will face. What I am suggesting is that by working with our thoughts and perceptions, we can better manage our experiences—not just in the moment but in the following hours, days, and weeks. Our lives and our work offer a wide spectrum of experience, so let's look at a very common example followed by a more complex one.

We'll start with something simple that many of us experience on a regular basis. Most of us live a life that is overscheduled—our days are filled with back-to-back appointments and responsibilities. A mishap like a traffic jam or a flat tire can ripple negatively through an entire day. We'll spend it running late for every appointment, apologizing for our tardiness, and feeling stressed and frustrated. Here's where our thought practice comes in. When triggering events happen, like a flat tire, our emotions can get the best of us and we can become angry, upset, and stressed. We may tense our bodies, use poor language, experience increased blood pressure or heart rates, and have all sorts of negative thoughts that spin uncontrollably in our minds. A single event can make us grumpy and resentful for an entire day.

Now consider this: How many decisions will we make during the day from this grumpy, angry place that we might have made differently if we were in a happy place? How are we showing up for our peers, our associates, our entire organization? Do we feel willing to serve from a headspace like this, or are we more likely to make quick decisions based on feelings of irritation, exasperation, or hurriedness? How might those different decisions have changed our day, our life, or the lives of others had we not been so frustrated when we made them? It's interesting to consider the ripple effect a single event can have, isn't it?

What alternative do we have? If we are using our thought practice and commitment to servant leadership, then when a stressful everyday event happens, we will notice when thoughts begin to spiral. We can slow our breathing, remembering these are just thoughts. We can refocus our minds on our broader goals, on our overall purpose, on those around us. None of the doomsday scenarios that the mind is chattering about have actually occurred, and there are countless possibilities for how this moment and the rest of our day can still be positive and turn out great.

We have the power to choose how we respond. We can begin to accept the fact that this event has occurred—we have a flat tire—and allow ourselves to feel a few moments of frustration. (Notice that our practice never involves avoiding or stifling our emotions. We cannot simply choose never to feel anything negative again; we just don't let ourselves get stuck in these lower-vibration emotions.) Then we can also begin to accept that our flat tire will have some sort of impact on our day; however, what that is remains to be seen. We are not foretelling doom and gloom or anticipating a downward spiral of annoyance.

From this space of acceptance and acknowledgment, we can now make the conscious choice not to let a flat tire ruin the next few hours (or beyond). We can choose not to let this mishap spread its negative impact throughout everything else that we do, leaving a wake of negative thinking and a lingering sour mood. Each time fear or worry starts to creep in, we can force a smile to our lips and affirm something positive, like this: *I am open to the possibility that everything is going to work out perfectly.*

I know some of you just read that sentence and said, "Okay, Jim. That sounds nice, but I have important meetings and being late could have significant consequences." I understand, but let's look at it logically. Notice that this affirmation doesn't state, "Everything is perfect, and I'm not bothered by this flat tire." This affirmation is guiding us to the possibility of perfection, allowing us to keep our minds open to another outcome.

Saying these words helps us interrupt our catastrophizing. It gives us the chance to avoid spiraling into assumptions about what this one small incident means for the rest of our day or even the whole week, month, or year. It shifts our perspective from one of disappointment or blame or persecution, and it puts us in a place of empowerment, a chance to see opportunities for action or improvement.

Would you rather try to overcome the circumstances of an unforeseen event from an angry, worried, stressed-out space, or are you willing to try something different? We often assume we have no control over our thoughts or feelings when something unexpected happens. But what if you tried—just once—a different kind of response, just to see what happens? Are you willing to respond by choosing to reorganize your day from a calmer place, a place where you have accepted your flat tire and are open to the possibility of everything working in a perfect way? Do you think that changing your mindset in this way will change how you approach the rest of your day?

Let's move on to a more complex scenario such as a job loss, an unforeseen change in circumstance, a personal illness, or one involving a family member or friend. I have experienced each of these difficult events very deeply at one time or another. There were times when I felt completely powerless and helpless about my own circumstances or those of a loved one. Extreme stress is inevitable in our lives. As difficult as it is, we must do our best to make choices about how we are experiencing extreme events.

We can manage our own thoughts. We must remember this and try to make choices about our thoughts, perceptions, and emotions in order to render the greatest service to ourselves and to our loved ones.

THE
FOUNDATIONAL
COMPONENT
OF BETTER
LIVING IS
MANAGING OUR
THOUGHTS AND
PERCEPTIONS.

We must allow ourselves to feel our emotions fully, but over and over we must also try to manage our thoughts and perceptions so they don't become fearful, negative, and worrisome. We must keep trying to turn to something that is either positive or at least neutral.

There will be scenarios where you just can't think of any positive thought to bring forth. That's okay. Do your best to muster up something neutral like, *This negative thinking is not serving me*, and just be in a neutral place. This may seem like too small a step to take, but it is critical to first get yourself out of that cycle of stress, fear, or negative thinking. Once you have achieved that step, you will be in a better position to provide yourself with the best mental and emotional state for healing. This may not put you suddenly in a place of acceptance or positivity, but it does open the door for those eventual states. You will also be in a clearer state for supporting loved ones who may also be moving through this difficult circumstance. Getting stuck in a negativity or stress loop won't be helpful to you or to them.

Over the course of many life experiences, I have learned something else that can help us. In every difficult experience I have struggled through, with the passage of time and hindsight, I have come to see a synchronicity, a blessing, have found clarity, and even seen in some cases why it could not have unfolded any other way. This has become so constant for me that I have leaned into it for comfort in difficult times. I can use my faculty of faith to know that although I am in the midst of pain and suffering, there will come a time when I will have greater understanding. This can help bring us peace.

The goal of our time here is to live happier, healthier, and more peaceful lives. The foundational component of better living is managing our thoughts and perceptions. Things are going to happen—negative things and good things too. This is the basis for the experience of life. Our responses to them shape our experience of life. From small to large, from inconsequential to monumental, with practice we can better choose how we are going to experience events rather than feeling tossed around by them.

We can't control all of life, but we don't have to feel powerless either. We can work with our thoughts, perceptions, and responses—starting with everyday events. The more in touch we become with our thoughts and perceptions, the more clarity we have to manage and change them positively, controlling our experiences in the short and long term.

Establishing a Culture of Trust

The importance of building a healthy and vibrant culture is that it creates an environment in which pursuing your mission is possible. Only in an atmosphere of trust, comfort, and appreciation will your associates feel committed to the broader goals of the organization. My experience has taught me five foundational elements required to build a thriving culture: putting people first, creating transparency, establishing trust and respect, prioritizing acknowledgment, and lightening up.

Element 1: Putting People First

Adopting a servant leadership philosophy begins the process of putting people first. However, there must be an active effort to demonstrate and model this priority consistently. It is critical that associates at all levels within the organization feel seen, heard, valued, and appreciated. There are numerous tactics and strategies for how to treat people well in business, which intersects again with our spiritual understanding. Oneness and practices such as the platinum (or golden) rule are timeless spiritual principles that embody this same element.

Element 2: Transparency

As we outlined earlier, transparency is paramount in any relationship. It is also essential as an element of culture development. Associates must feel they can express themselves freely without repercussions, and at the same time, they must feel the information they receive from the organization is truthful and sincere. We already know honesty and transparency as spiritual principle. Consider Ephesians 4:25: "So then, putting away falsehood, let all of us speak the truth to our neighbors, for we are members of one another." The scripture not only reinforces the call for transparency but emphasizes the spiritual principle of oneness. The Buddha is credited with saying, "The gift of truth excels all other gifts." This honest level of communication between an organization and its associates is foundational in a culture and also builds a platform for the next element.

Element 3: Trust and Respect

Transparency is essential in building a flourishing culture, because establishing trust and respect is built upon this bedrock. Look at any healthy relationship you have ever had or witnessed. At the core of its success, you will always find there was mutual trust and respect. Both are built upon the foundation of transparency and grow out of a dedication to treating people with respect and dignity. From Romans 12:10 (NIV), "Be devoted to one another in love. Honor one another above yourselves." Every person and position in the organization is to be valued and respected. The great Mahatma Gandhi tells us, "Relationships are based on four principles: respect, understanding, acceptance, and appreciation." If this can be accomplished, the organizational culture is entrenched in healthy interpersonal and group relationships that embody success and are in direct alignment with spiritual principle.

ACKNOWLEDGING ASSOCIATES CAN BE INCORPORATED EASILY INTO THE SPIRITUAL PRACTICE OF GRATITUDE.

Element 4: Acknowledgment

Once an organization has created transparency with its associates and developed healthy trust and respect, one of the most overlooked elements in today's workforce must then be employed. It is the process of intently and consistently acknowledging associates and their good work. A 2013 study from *Psychology Today* reported that 83 percent of respondents said recognition for contributions was more fulfilling than any reward or gift. Let that sink in for a moment, particularly if you often assume acknowledgment requires its own line in your budget. The study also showed that 76 percent found peer praise very or extremely motivating and 88 percent found praise from managers very or extremely motivating.

Acknowledging associates can be incorporated easily into the spiritual practice of gratitude. Simply expressing gratitude on a regular basis increases morale and productivity. At Unity Village, our entire executive team participates in what we call Walkabout Wednesday. It is the practice of taking 30 minutes every Wednesday to walk around to different areas of campus, thanking team members for their service and contributions. It was a tradition held by the Fillmores, the founders of Unity, and we brought it back in 2017. This simple act has been instrumental in changing the culture at the Village. Not surprisingly, spiritual principle tells us that whatever we are grateful for increases, which easily explains the increases in productivity and morale.

Element 5: Lighten Up

Too often the environments where people serve, be they for-profit or for-cause, have too much formality, seriousness, pressure, and stress embedded in their culture. I understand it's work, not recess, yet recent studies show that the more relaxed, joyful, and satisfied associates are, the more productive they are. A 2018 study by *talent-works.com* shows that happy employees experience 31 percent higher productivity. In addition, Talent Works studies show happy employees are 37 percent better at sales and three times more creative than their unhappy counterparts. This data clearly tells us that businesses and their leaders need to lighten up a little and focus more on associate happiness and relationship building.

What does that look like in today's work world? Below are some steps to support an engaged and supportive culture.

Guidelines, Not Rules. It starts at the beginning when an associate is hired and is first introduced to your organization's policies and procedures. You can tell a lot about a company and its culture by the way Human Resources' materials are written. Is the language patronizing or unyielding? Or is it written as if we are all adults, presenting recommended guidelines? Of course, legalities require the establishment of solid processes, rules, and procedures, but the way they are presented communicates the spirit of intention behind them. A tone that is parental and punitive often elicits resistance, while language that is clear yet supportive fosters an environment of cooperation. Whether you are onboarding associates, volunteers, or even contractors, this is an opportunity to set the tenor of both accountability and clear expectations while modeling the culture you are creating through the tone of the language used.

Social Engagement. The backbone of any healthy culture is relationships. Whether peer-to-peer or leaders-to-staff, people at work are in relationship with one another. The way to foster meaningful and healthy relationships is to create opportunities for people to relax and get to know one another outside of work. Creating events for socializing fosters these important relationships while allowing associates to relax and begin to think of work as more than just, well, work.

Too often, social gatherings in traditional business settings are discounted and deemed a waste of time. However, recent survey data and research (some of it quoted earlier) shows that the opposite is true: Social engagement equals personal engagement, which leads to a healthier and more productive team. One of the best examples of this can be found in ministry. Churches and ministries have a great grasp of this concept in the form of fellowship and potluck gatherings. These staples of Sunday social connection have been used to foster greater engagement and community for generations. It deepens personal relationships while at the same time fostering connection with the organization.

Fun. Don't be afraid to let employees have fun at work. Sure, we must maintain professionalism, and there are times for serious discussions and focus. But in between those times, let your associates know they can have fun *and* be productive. The payoff will be more relaxed, joyful, and productive team members. And much like providing opportunities for social gatherings above, it supports and sustains engagement for your team as a whole. For example, some of the things we are doing for this in the Unity culture include quarterly socials, employee picnics, a massive Christmas party that associates look forward to all year long, a Halloween costume contest (even online), and holiday competitions between departments. Once I even bought our creative department some mini drones to fly around in their new open floor plan space.

Employing these five fundamental elements in an organization's culture—putting people first, creating transparency, establishing trust and respect, prioritizing acknowledgment, and lightening up—will add meaningful depth to an associate's experience at work and will create an environment that is both productive and supportive to the overall well-being of those who serve there. In his book *Jesus Christ Heals*, Unity cofounder Charles Fillmore says, "We all should practice delightful, happy, joyous states of mind. It is such thoughts that open the way for the ever-present Father-Mind to pour out its splendid resources into our mind and through us into all our affairs." The happier and healthier the individuals are serving in an organization, the more productive and healthier the organization will be overall.

Overcoming False Perceptions

Many of the concepts outlined previously are foreign to the traditional business environment. They may even seem counterintuitive. As leadership and cultural norms evolve, so must our individual perceptions. One important way to make space for change in our worldview is understanding how we perceive the environment around us.

Perception is loosely defined as the process of interpreting stimuli. However, interpretation of any stimulus is always accompanied by reference to our past experiences. For example, someone who has never seen an automobile would be unable to identify one, but a person who had seen automobiles before would be able to identify it easily. Hence, perception may then be wholly defined as a process of interpreting a present stimulus based on past experiences. Why is this understanding of perception relevant and meaningful? It helps us to better understand the part it plays in our daily experience. Because the truth is, based on our definition here, *everything we witness and take in through our five senses is filtered through our past experiences.* And why is that so important? Because sometimes our past experiences and conditioned, preconceived judgments can lead us to misinterpret or misjudge present moment experiences.

Consider the famous experiment described by Gene Weingarten in a 2007 *Washington Post* article, "Pearls Before Breakfast." Joshua Bell, a world-renowned musician, quietly surfaced from the subway in Washington, D.C., unkempt in a T-shirt, jeans, and ball cap, and proceeded to play for more than 40 minutes on a priceless Stradivarius violin. His performance went largely unnoticed while more than 1,000 people passed by, dropping just over $30 in a cup. How many of those same 1,000 people would have or may have in the past shelled out more than $100 per ticket to watch this same man play? Were they led astray by their perception about people who play on the street? Or was it their perception about his appearance? In this example, it would seem that past experiences related to street musicians led to a missed opportunity to have a better-than-front-row experience listening to a premier violinist demonstrating his craft for a mere donation.

Now consider a more practical example. Let's say that our office hours begin at 8 a.m. We encounter a coworker who consistently shows up at 8:15. Our past experience has taught us to always follow the rules and be on time. As a result, our perception of this

IT IS
TREMENDOUSLY
HELPFUL
TO KNOW
YOUR OWN
PERCEPTION
BIASES AND
TRIGGERS.

coworker may not be positive since everyone else on the team seems to be able to honor the 8 a.m. start time. However, would we perceive the situation differently if we knew she was a single parent with a child whose school doesn't open until 8 a.m.—and that she has made special arrangements with her supervisor to make up the time by staying late? We never have the whole story.

As you can see, we must carefully monitor our perceptions of present moment experiences lest we miss once-in-a-lifetime opportunities or harshly and undeservedly misjudge people around us, both known and unknown. It is essential to put our meditation and awareness practices to use in understanding our own experiences, but it's just as important to recognize how much we miss when it comes to those around us.

Sadly, perception is likely the source of more than half of all miscommunications in relationships of every kind. You see, our individual past experiences can become triggers for how we interpret tone, specific words, or even phrases that may bring up painful memories from our past. Accordingly, we must always be mindful of separating this present moment experience from those unrelated experiences in the past. Otherwise, we risk visiting and assigning a range of historical reactions to the present moment that don't belong.

For this reason, it is tremendously helpful to know your own perception biases and triggers. Becoming aware of them creates opportunities to challenge them, rather than unwittingly giving into them time after time.

If we no longer agree with what we first perceived, we can change our minds.

Part of managing our perception is what we have been discussing, simply the awareness that we carry our unique lens of the world from our lived experiences into every interaction. The other key component then is to be open to seeing every experience as it is *without* including our instant judgments. To do so we must be open and willing to see things differently while remaining curious about each situation as it unfolds. We have to bring with us a healthy sense of wonder to every interaction and experience—wondering how it is different from our experience, wondering how it may unfold, and wondering what we may learn from it. This practice will help us be more present with each new experience we encounter while embracing the possibility of a new perspective.

Inviting Everyone to the Table

As we have discussed in previous chapters, change is more than just inevitable; it's also critical to making the shifts we need to see in the world. The United States has struggled to come to terms with the realities of racial inequity and the impact of systemized discrimination of marginalized populations. During the past few years in particular, there has been a greater awakening to this reality (although we have a long way to go), and many organizations are making a serious push toward formal diversity, equity, and inclusion programs.

This is an important step in our efforts to create a just and equitable society, one in which every person feels seen, heard, and valued. We are working toward a world in which there is an understanding that everyone's lived experience is not the same and in which we have compassion for each other regardless of that fact. To truly have a healthy culture in any organization, large or small, every person must feel safe and accepted and respected.

To achieve that, robust DEI (diversity, equity, and inclusion) programs are essential. These programs must provide training for all associates on topics like racism, social justice, privilege, microaggressions, and unconscious bias. These ongoing trainings and conversations will help increase the cultural competency and sensitivity in your teams, improving the work experience for current employees in your organization. It can also help you begin to attract a more diverse workforce, encouraging candidates to apply with confidence that they will be welcomed, respected, and valued for who they are—and comfortable and safe in your workplace and organizational culture.

When I was applying for the Unity CEO role, I took great pains to prepare for the two-day interview process.

I prepared a presentation for my innovative ideas to help stabilize and grow every area of the organization. I had a comprehensive strategy for how to create a more engaged and productive culture. I felt as ready as I ever have for any interview. Then two-thirds of the way through the second day, one of the board members asked a question I had not prepared for. It was a simple, straightforward question that caught me by surprise. Keep in mind this was in 2016 before the recent rise in awareness and acceptance of diversity programs on such a wide scale. She said, "How will you address the absence of people of color and different nationalities in our organization?"

I had spent decades in the IT industry, where there was an abundance of global diversity, so this was not an issue I had faced before. I was moved deeply as she described her difficult experiences with a lack of diversity and inclusion in this organization. A few weeks after I started, I realized just how much we lacked diversity on campus. I was also becoming more and more aware of how difficult it is for marginalized populations to succeed in our country, and I was waking up to the systemic ideologies that are slanted toward the white population. It began to be clear to me that we were out of alignment with what Unity stood for, and I was going to have to make this a greater priority.

I received a second nudge from an associate who approached me after my first all-employee meeting. She shared with me her love for Unity and our organization

WE NEEDED TO CHANGE OUR CULTURE SO EVERYONE FELT SEEN, HEARD, AND APPRECIATED FOR WHO THEY WERE.

but then went on to express her concern that there were not more people on campus who looked like her. Furthermore, she shared with me that her lived experience on campus as a person of color wasn't always pleasant. This was a huge disappointment to me. It really told me that we needed to change our culture so everyone felt seen, heard, and appreciated for who they were.

Working with our chief people officer, we began to take basic steps toward creating a DEI program. Very quickly we realized how much help we needed. Within 18 months we had hired a full-time DEI strategist who was committed to helping us with the following:

1. Improve the diversity at our headquarters campus.
2. Create an environment where everyone feels welcomed and appreciated.
3. Create lasting change that will improve the lived experience for marginalized and oppressed populations in the Unity sphere of influence.

Our I.D.E.A. (inclusion, diversity, equity, and acceptance) program, under the guidance of this expert in the field, has flourished, and we have taken steps toward all three of the above goals. This work is constantly evolving but with a singular focus in mind: to create an inclusive environment that encourages our team members and stakeholders to show up as their authentic selves in a comfortable way.

To be truly successful, these programs must provide a commitment to a more diverse workforce. This increases opportunities for marginalized populations and creates a ripple effect of positive change in the world. Leverage your leadership to inspire change within your sphere of influence for the greater good. If more organizations are operating this way, great change will take place. In the future, your prospective associates will see people who look like them in your workforce, trusting it is safe for them to be there and thus creating momentum in your efforts to be more diverse.

My sincere hope is that these human factors are enough to motivate leaders to take up the mantle for DEI. For those who require more data related to overall company performance and success metrics, consider these statistics from a 2021 article at *whattobecome.com*:

- Inclusive companies are more likely to lead and capture new markets.
- 43 percent of companies with diverse management exhibit higher profits.
- Companies with racial and ethnic diversity are 35 percent more likely to perform at a higher level and have increased return on investment (ROI).
- Diverse teams are 87 percent better decision-makers than individuals.

- Highly inclusive companies are more likely to hit their financial target goals by up to 120 percent.
- Racially diverse teams provide 35 percent better performance compared to their competitors.
- Companies with high racial diversity see *15 times* more revenue and sales.

You can't argue with those numbers. It is clear that comprehensive DEI programs can be both a spiritual practice with humanitarian benefits and a business practice with a positive impact on your bottom line. It's absolutely worth investing your resources to help create a healthier culture, a more successful business, and a world that works for all.

Innovating Continuously

I have had the great fortune of working for multiple market-leading companies in my career. I took advantage of these opportunities to learn the "secret formula" for how these companies were able to maintain their positions at the top. There were two common ingredients among these highly successful businesses. The first was a commitment to finding highly capable

THE STANDARDS WE UPHOLD OR THE ACTIONS WE TAKE DEVELOP A HISTORICAL SIGNIFICANCE, AND THEY MAY BECOME SACRED COWS.

people. Each of those top companies was dedicated to the practice of recruiting and retaining the best available talent within their means—and then nurturing that talent while letting them be the experts in their assigned roles. In other words, surround yourself with people who are smarter than you in their respective areas of expertise, then empower them with the authority and freedom to make decisions and execute in their roles and responsibilities.

The second common ingredient in these leading companies was a formalized commitment to ongoing innovation. They were committed to continuous improvement in their processes, procedures, operations, and, of course, their product and service offerings. They had means, measures, and formal processes for capturing every single new idea—no matter how small—vetting it, and either implementing or discarding it depending on viability and return. This consistent willingness to change and improve is what separates and sustains market leaders from those that become stagnant and begin to decline.

There is much we can learn from this practice of continuous evolution. Most of us on a spiritual path spend years studying, evolving, and constantly trying to become a greater expression of the Divine. Often, we experience great periods of growth intertwined with occasional setbacks. It rarely evolves linearly or predictably. Over time, and with wisdom, we have learned this is simply part of our journey.

But when it comes to applying this practice in nonprofit organizations and endeavors, especially those that are spiritually inclined, there's a tendency to give up our willingness to innovate through trial and error. This rarely seems to be a conscious or intentional decision, but it can be very easy for processes to slip into traditions. The standards we uphold or the actions we take develop a historical significance, and they may even become sacred cows. We find ourselves insisting, "This is how we do things," without giving a second thought to why that is or whether it still serves us as well as it could (or should). This can lead to months and even years when our practices and offerings become stagnant. Beneath it all is an undercurrent of resistance to change—sometimes conscious, sometimes unconscious. Unfortunately, this desire to remain comfortable and avoid a constant commitment to change can lead to less-than-optimal results for the mission or business we are serving.

An inability to change can sneak up on us, especially because there are many reasons why an organization may stop pursuing change. Sometimes we just get comfortable; it doesn't even occur to us to question the current status or consider making a shift. If our organization has faced big challenges in the past, finding a period of success can lead to grasping tightly to those wins rather than seeing it as part of a broader trend. In fact, some organizations cut their potential success short with a scarcity mindset; they reach a plateau in their growth and decide not to push their "luck" any further, limiting their own capacity for abundance.

A commitment to continuous improvement is necessary for any organization to remain healthy and relevant. This means a constant search to get better in processes, procedures, products, culture, and so on. It takes effort and practice, but constantly evaluating what, how, and why things are done in an organization can lead to an infinite number of positive changes and consistent growth over time. This constant evolution toward improvement almost assures longevity and sustainability. In nature we know that if something is stagnant or not growing, it is likely dying. We must avoid stagnation in every facet of our organizations lest we begin the process of decline.

Gems from Part Three: Evolving Leadership

- A common leadership philosophy needs to be shared among all your leaders so employees will have consistent experiences from department to department.

- Styles of fear and intimidation or command and control may get short-term results, but they stifle innovation, input, and creativity.

- Servant leadership is a blend of spiritual principles and best practices for business. The focus is on supporting and appreciating your people, while exercising empathy and compassion.

- My tenets of servant leadership are to prioritize people, create transparency, focus on the future, and be compassionate in all things.

- People are different! They hear and process information differently. Learn about and accommodate various styles of behavior and decision-making.

- You have the power to choose your thoughts and experience. That means you can decide how you show up, even on a difficult day. A flat tire doesn't have to ruin your day, and you don't have to ruin the days of others.

- If you can't be positive, at least work up to neutral.

- Remember all the times when a difficult experience yielded blessings and clarity over time. Have faith it will again.

- Five Elements to Establish a Culture of Trust

    1. Put people first: Everyone in the organization needs to feel seen, heard, valued, and appreciated.
    2. Be transparent: Associates must feel free to express themselves without repercussions and also feel the information they are receiving from the organization is truthful and sincere.
    3. Trust and respect others: This is the basis of any good relationship.
    4. Acknowledge good work: Recognition is more fulfilling than any gift or reward.
    5. Lighten up: Create guidelines instead of rules, host social events, and have some fun while doing the work.

- Many of our opinions and judgments are merely perceptions that are not completely accurate or are triggered by baggage from the past. Be open to seeing every person and experience as it is, without instant judgment. Stay curious as each situation unfolds.

- Invite everyone to the table. Programs for diversity, equity, and inclusion are essential for all associates. Company performance soars with diverse teams.
- Commit to innovation—continuous improvement in everything you do. Stay open to every new idea. It's easy to get stuck in being comfortable, doing the same thing year after year.

PART FOUR

Handling Change, Crisis, and Failure

Making Change Your Friend

Even when we feel most grounded and competent, the unexpected is inevitable. We face sudden change, endure crises, and experience failures. These can be minor setbacks or unthinkable tragedies. No matter how prepared we are (or how prepared we *think* we are), we will find ourselves unbalanced from time to time.

We have talked a lot here about new concepts, new perceptions, and a constant call for change. This may induce anxiety for some. I know it's not easy, but it is important. Here is something interesting for you to consider; I dare say it may blow your mind. One ancient teaching can dramatically shift the course of your life every single day. It is the simplest practice we have discussed since we started our journey together. That's right, it is both the simplest practice and can have the single biggest impact on your day-to-day experience. It is this: Make change your friend.

Let me say it again. We need to make friends with the fact that everything in life changes. Why? Nothing in life—in our lives, other people's lives, nature, or anywhere you look—will ever, ever remain static. At some point everything will change. It is universal law. It has been happening for billions of years in the natural world and it happens in our families, jobs, businesses, neighborhoods, and so on. Change is required in the spiritual process of transformation.

Either fortunately or unfortunately, to everything there is a season. Sometimes change is terribly painful in our experience, like the death of a friend, family member, or pet. Sometimes it is joyful, such as an exciting new job or getting married or having a baby. Other times change is the welcome result of moving through a particularly difficult period—recovering from an illness, a divorce, or healing from an injury. What I want you to consider are all those daily, weekly, monthly, run-of-the-mill changes that are going to occur in life. They that aren't life-threatening, but they are still a part of the evolution of life.

First, let's own up to the fact that many of us just don't like change. But unless we want to spend our lives constantly disappointed, we must begin to accept that some level of change is going to happen in our lives pretty regularly. This will begin to bring some mental peace. Second, for the changes we really don't like—and here is the terribly unfortunate kicker—most of us dig in and create our own mental and emotional suffering by reacting negatively and having what is usually a very unconstructive reaction. In truth, what we didn't want to change did exactly what it can't help but do: It changed. We can spin in our own negativity about this change for very long periods of time. Often, we tell anyone and everyone who will listen how unhappy we are about this change—a reorganization at work, a loved one moving far away, a new business coming to the neighborhood, and so on. This just prolongs our mental and emotional anguish.

Most of the time, this resistance does nothing but create suffering. This is why recognizing that the world is going to evolve and change—and making change our friend—is so profound. It allows us to completely release the need to resist change and instead be emotionally and mentally open to changing with the world around us as it evolves.

I don't know about you, but I would like to be as welcoming to every change in my life as I am to springtime after a long, harsh winter. I think I would be far less stressed and worried, and far happier and more peaceful, if this were my approach to all the change that is inevitable in life. Don't get me wrong, there are times for proper resistance—in addressing social justice issues, or changes that impact a population negatively, for example—I am not referring to those sorts of things here. I am referring to our own individual, mental, and emotional resistance to change when the entire world is going to change no matter what we do.

So why not consider an alternative approach? Why not make change our friend? If we do, we will dramatically reduce our own mental and emotional stress, and we will evolve into that which is new much more easily and quickly, without disturbance to our internal well-being.

Earlier, I mentioned that when I was recruited to join the energy management company in 2011, the

RESISTANCE DOES NOTHING BUT CREATE SUFFERING.

team was less than excited about the culture of change I wanted to develop. "I don't blame them," you're probably thinking. "Change can be threatening." But as we continued to repeat that affirmation, *Change is our friend*, a shift occurred. The team stopped merely tolerating this call to action and began to actually embrace change. After a few months, the group had developed a new sense of resiliency; they began looking beyond the changes I was implementing as their leader to offer their own innovative suggestions for improvement. Our mission was to address the service levels that had fallen in recent years, creating IT best practices that had been neglected because most of their previous leaders had utility backgrounds rather than information technology expertise. We succeeded in turning the operation around and after just a couple of years were receiving industry recognition and customer accolades for our service and support.

When I left five years later to return to Unity, my team—more than 100 people—secured an electric meter as a going-away present for me. Each person signed it, and they had installed a gold plaque on the front that read: "Change is our friend."

Changing our mindset to embrace change (or, at bare minimum, accept it) helps us minimize our mental and emotional suffering, both as individuals and as a group. One of the best ways leaders of organizations or ministries can manage the change process is to mentally and emotionally prepare their teams for the changes up front using transparent communications and tools and techniques that positively reinforce the acceptance of those changes.

Recognizing Resistance

A practice of acceptance is essential to having a clear mind that supports our well-being both professionally and personally. So let's talk about how to recognize resistance. If you are a sci-fi fan, you will be familiar with the oft-quoted saying, "Resistance is futile" from the *Star Trek: The Next Generation* series. I wonder whether the writers understood they were peppering the world with an ancient universal truth as well as a powerful life lesson. You see, resistance to anything that has shown up in our lives really *is* futile. Whatever is before us has already occurred, and there is nothing we can do in this moment to change the fact that this circumstance is now here.

This is where it gets troublesome. The natural human instinct is to resist anything we don't want in our lives. As a result, our minds begin to chatter, and often we create our own suffering for hours and sometimes days because we are unhappy with the current situation. We expend copious amounts of time and energy agonizing over the unwanted situation, wishing things were different,

WE REALLY
CANNOT
CHANGE WHAT
IS BEFORE US.
HOWEVER, WE
CAN CHANGE
EVERYTHING
THAT HAPPENS
AFTER AN
UNWANTED
CIRCUMSTANCE
SHOWS UP.

complaining, and suffering mentally and emotionally in an effort to resist what is. Resistance is futile because we really cannot change what is before us. However, we can change everything that happens after an unwanted circumstance shows up.

This is where the practice of acceptance comes in. Many people misinterpret the meaning of *acceptance* by assuming we just become doormats to life, accepting every circumstance that shows up, and giving up our power to do anything. That is not at all what this practice is about. It is quite the opposite. *Acceptance* means focusing on solutions. The power and practice of acceptance is a method for allowing us to move beyond the needless suffering of the experience and move more quickly to focus on positive action steps to deal with our circumstances.

Here's an example: Let's combine our mind, energy, and emotions, and think of them as a computer processing engine. Let's pretend that each day we have a limited amount of processing power in this computer processor. As luck would have it, an unwanted circumstance shows up in our experience—a problem at home, something goes wrong at work—you choose the scenario. The moment this unwanted situation shows up, we have two options for using the limited power in our computer processor. We can spend our power in a state of denial and resistance, complaining and agonizing *or* we can quickly accept what is and use our minds, energy, and emotions to focus on how we can solve or move through this experience without the needless suffering our minds generally create for us.

The practice of acceptance is not about lying down and letting life events run over us, but rather minimizing the time wasted in resisting those unwanted events. When we minimize our own internal chatter and suffering about such events, we can move quickly to the next steps to move past them. We can choose to accept a situation, even though we would have preferred something else to happen and focus our attention on putting a more preferable experience in its place.

There is an old saying, "Change is never painful; only the resistance to change is painful." It is important for us to note that even with the practice of acceptance, some life events—although we are not resisting—still can and will be painful. Serious health issues in ourselves or our loved ones, death or any major loss, changes in circumstances, heartbreaks—they can all result in emotional or physical pain. The caution here is that pain and suffering are not the same thing unless we are in a state of resistance. The healthiest approach is to be completely open to the truth of what we are experiencing, fully feel and express our emotions (don't suppress them), and allow them to flow through us.

It is perfectly normal and healthy to express our emotions about serious life events. Our practice is to minimize the resistance and struggle by focusing on positive and healthy steps to recovery and dealing with

THE PRACTICE OF ACCEPTANCE IS NOT ABOUT LYING DOWN AND LETTING LIFE EVENTS RUN OVER US, BUT MINIMIZING THE TIME WASTED IN RESISTING.

these events. The next time an unwanted circumstance shows up in your life or your work, try this: Pause, take a deep breath, and be thoughtful about where you choose to spend your time, emotion, and energy. What if you react to mishaps, mistakes, and misunderstandings with a state of acceptance—focused on next steps instead of returning again and again to what has already occurred? This approach can help you move forward, feeling healthier, happier, and more peaceful in your life and work.

Approaching Challenges with Peace

While serving in one of the more highly visible roles in my career I had occasion to practice peace firsthand. In this particular instance, myself, my boss, our CEO, and several other high-level leadership team members from our organization were called to a client site. We were all there to address some perceived lingering failures in a particular area of our hosted software platform. This was one of the largest clients in North America, and they wielded a great deal of negotiating power when it came to both the current and future capabilities of our platform. They contributed tens of millions of dollars to our annual revenue.

This particular meeting was going to be tense—probably very tense. Their interpretation of the data gathered to explore this problem was not in alignment with our interpretation of the data. We were there to defend our position and to come to some sort of understanding as to how to move forward—all, we hoped, without doing any damage to the long-term relationship with this client. There were a lot of big titles and big egos in the room.

During my time working toward my Master of Divinity degree, I had acquired useful skills related to nonviolent communication, deep listening, and unattached, present moment awareness. As the chosen leader of this meeting from our side, I had the responsibility of leading the dialogue, presenting our findings, and managing the flow of communication throughout the meeting. Given the divergent viewpoints on what was causing the system errors, there were several occasions in which a leader from one side or the other would escalate the debate with a raised voice and even, sometimes, accusatory statements. Each time this happened, I would calmly and politely restate what I thought I heard and then ask for someone from the other side to respond. I was careful never to let anyone from the other side respond immediately to one of these escalated statements, not without my interjection and a resetting of the tone prior to the response. The meeting was tense, but this kept the discussion cordial and professional.

OUR SKILLS IN RESPONDING TO THE OUTER WORLD FROM A CENTER OF PEACE CAN HELP US BE MORE PRODUCTIVE THAN WE EVER THOUGHT WE COULD BE.

In the end, we managed to have a thorough conversation about the circumstances. Each side felt heard. Responsibility was ultimately accepted on both sides, as both organizations had contributed to the ongoing system problems. A long-term approach for moving forward was agreed upon. My ability to manage my own thoughts and emotions, despite feeling triggered multiple times by some of the accusations hurled directly at my team, afforded me the opportunity to create a space for myself and the others in the room to work through a very difficult set of circumstances in a relatively peaceful and calm manner.

Upon the conclusion of the meeting, our team was walking to dinner as a group. The North American CEO for our company approached me with a somewhat puzzled look on his face. He congratulated me for a job well done and complimented my ability to navigate that discussion without the drama and boisterous disagreement that can happen in those settings. He said to me, "You know, since I first met you, I have been watching you. Given your size, stature, and presence, I was very excited. I was sure I was getting a linebacker who would not be intimidated and could effectively lead this part of our business. But instead, we seemed to have hired a Zen Buddhist." I wasn't quite sure how to take that comment. Before I could make up my mind how to respond, he went on to assure me that he was not disappointed in me and, in fact, just the opposite. He had never seen a meeting like the one we'd just been through managed in such a way that aggressive disagreement wasn't a factor.

The moral of the story is that our ability to control and manage our own thoughts and emotions can yield far more effective results. Our skills in responding to the outer world from a center of peace, without the mental and emotional disturbance of ourselves or others, can help us be more productive than we ever thought we could be. Using many of the techniques and practices we have discussed in the previous chapters, we can and ultimately will reach a state where our thoughts and emotions can be more easily controlled, and we can respond to the outer world from a posture of peace, acceptance, and presence.

Being Prepared for Anything

I'm often asked about this positive approach of using affirmations and the idea that we create our experiences through our thoughts, words, and actions—and how that applies in contingency planning for a business. After all, the two do seem to be at odds with each other at first glance. How do we create contingency plans in case the business begins to struggle or draw up a disaster recovery plan without putting all our attention and energy toward the very thing we are trying to avoid?

PREPARATION WORKS BEST WHEN YOU PREPARE FOR BOTH THE WORST-CASE SCENARIOS *AND* THE BEST-CASE OUTCOMES.

In my experience, and as we discussed earlier, it is easy for the mind to begin spiraling among all the negative things that could happen. Fear can quickly take hold and the worst possible outcomes can begin to dominate the consciousness of a team.

To help combat this tendency, I have learned that preparation works best when you prepare for both the worst-case scenarios *and* the best-case outcomes. While you create plans for those less-than-optimal scenarios, also make it a priority to spend time creating a vision for the most desirable scenarios. This offers a sense of balance to the process, and it also prevents teams from completely spiraling out in fear or panic that the worst is inevitable.

Possible outcomes for any given process or project often fall along a spectrum, and rarely is the actual outcome at one end or the other. Instead, we usually end up somewhere in the middle between perfection and catastrophe. But we often only plan for catastrophe. Preparing for both the positive and the negative seems to allow people to detach from the circumstances and scenarios, making it possible to release the emotional grip on a specific plan and begin to see it as an exercise in preparation. Just as we plan and prepare for our strategic vision or the success we desire, we can do the same for difficult scenarios (and without investing our energy solely in the outcomes we want to avoid).

In my role as CEO, I'm asked each year to update our contingency plans for the steps we would take if organizational finances reached a particularly low threshold. Each year before we review the plans, our team affirms that we will never need this document, but it is still a prudent and necessary step in the reality of running a business. It would be irresponsible not to create such plans, putting the organization and the work we do at risk should something unplanned occur. Instead, we engage in this planning process, documenting the logical steps that would be taken if needed.

I don't worry about "giving too much energy" to emergency financial plans because we follow it up with an exercise to plan for optimal financial outcomes. We plan for what happens when everything goes *right*, whether it's a revision to the strategic plan, identifying new opportunities for growth, or looking for ways to improve our culture. Structuring our contingency planning work this way, with both a positive beginning and ending, helps us feel prepared no matter what happens while directing our time, energy, and consciousness into the growth opportunities that would sustain and enhance our work.

Whenever scenarios show up in a business or ministry that can cause associates, congregants, or stakeholders to become consumed with worry, our responsibility as leaders is to help them focus on a positive direction that is counter to the circumstances generating fear. Allowing uncertainty or concern to fester can cause panic to spread. Instead, remind your organization that you're prepared to handle anything, and show them you're confident things will soon go right.

Navigating Setbacks

We may have mastered a sense of stasis in our typical days, but what happens when something goes wrong personally or professionally? You finally have your sleep routine down, then new neighbors with a barking dog move in. You start treating your body like a friend instead of an enemy, then you get a scary diagnosis. You find a rhythm at work, then a pandemic sweeps the globe. Sometimes these setbacks can be overcome with a deep breath and a reminder that our circumstances are always temporary. Sometimes, however, navigating what may appear as a crisis can quickly feel overwhelming.

Every one of us will experience loss, suffering, or difficult struggles of some kind during our lifetimes. Though inevitable, this hurt is no less painful. How do we manage in those difficult times? What is the answer to navigating the most challenging parts of our journey?

In my own experience, there is no secret formula. What I have found to be most helpful is to hold fast to the same principles and teachings we have identified in this book to help us stay centered in troubling times.

TOO OFTEN IN TURMOIL OR CRISIS, WE STEP AWAY FROM THE HABITS AND PRACTICES THAT HAVE HELPED US, WHEN IN TRUTH WE NEED THEM MOST DURING DIFFICULT TIMES.

We continue (or even increase) our commitment to our spiritual practice and the habits we have formed to develop the best version of our daily lives. This must be true even while creating space to process feelings of loss, grief, or anger when they arise. Letting go of our fears or resentments or concerns about the future and of what *could* happen isn't easy, but it is essential.

Too often in turmoil or crisis, we step away from all the habits and practices that have helped us navigate the day-to-day, when in truth we need them most during difficult times. If we haven't managed our mindset on the days without any crises, how can we expect to respond when there's something scary or worrisome going on? Our minds take us to the worst possible scenarios, creating dramatic and awful outcomes for even the most mundane circumstances. This may be a very common trick of the human mind but living there will only bring greater suffering. When we let our minds jump to conclusions—especially the worst-case scenarios—we lose track of what is actually happening in our lives. Getting caught up in trying to control the narrative of the future is often a coping mechanism, whether we're doing it consciously or not. Predicting what could happen is a way to feel less helpless or powerless. However, this need to control or change the situation can be our greatest enemy in these circumstances.

The unfortunate consequence is that this can create a self-fulfilling prophecy. If our thoughts create our experiences, dwelling on these negative outcomes can influence our lived experience. I have learned that it helps to focus instead only on the things we can control. Sometimes these are small choices, but they can help us feel as if we have some impact on what's happening, can help restore some sense of power to our being, and can provide an influence toward the best outcome. This ensures we're keeping our attention on what can be done and our energy moving toward the positive choices that support our mission or goals in life. This is immensely important to our mental and emotional states as we move through the peaks and valleys, the joys and sorrows, of life.

Facing Personal Tragedy or Loss

I have found over and over that there are really no words, spiritual teachings, or practices that can take away our pain and suffering when tragedy finds its way into our life. When we are experiencing great loss, there is little to be done except to feel our grief and our anguish. What I have learned is that we must be present with and experience our pain fully and out loud. Science and psychology both tell us this is the healthiest way to process our pain, as this approach to embracing the hurt keeps us from storing unprocessed thoughts, feelings, and emotions. When we're able to express all three, it provides an opportunity to move through them instead of becoming stuck in our suffering.

This is where a professional counselor can be especially helpful. This process can feel lonely, isolating, and overwhelming, but we can enlist a therapist, analyst, or coach to assist in this journey. Finding a neutral party who has the skills to help us process our experience is like creating a safe space. There, we can explore our thoughts and feelings with support, helping us develop a sense of peace—even amid our darkest pain. Getting support during a journey of grief is absolutely the best thing we can do to ensure our well-being through the difficulties and challenges we face.

This really becomes our goal with any personal crisis or loss: to walk the path and come out the other side having done everything we can to ensure both our short- and long-term well-being. Though it won't eliminate our suffering, it will help us protect our mind, body, and spirit as best we can while navigating the valleys of life.

It also provides an opportunity to deepen our empathy with others. After all, we will all face heartbreak and pain at some time or another. When I have experienced deep loss, I have often felt a reminder tugging on my heart that while the circumstances might be unique to me, grief is a universal emotion. My awareness of how many people are living in pain proved to be a catalyst

WE MUST BE PRESENT WITH AND EXPERIENCE OUR PAIN FULLY AND OUT LOUD.

for my commitment to help and serve others, exactly what Unity is positioned to do through our ministries, publications, and resources.

It is critical for any of us, in the midst of our crises (or the crises of a loved one), to find something consistent that provides space between us and the circumstances. Prayer, exercise, movies, books, a creative practice—anything that allows for some space and a break from the situation. This small, consistent respite will help keep us centered and grounded, and it can help relieve the cycle of stress and worry. It helps to take us out of our heads and to feel normal, even if only for a few moments. This is necessary for our mental and emotional well-being as we try to keep our footing in the day-to-day experience of life.

Leading Through Painful Circumstances

We can also face crises in our roles as leaders. The Covid-19 pandemic is a fitting example. Because we have chosen the path of leadership, it is our responsibility to think first of our associates, customers, or congregants and of the well-being of the organization. This is a daily expectation for leaders, of course, but it becomes truly critical in times of crisis.

First and foremost, as we have discussed previously, our best chance for success as both leaders and individuals is to perform at our optimum level. This does not mean we operate at the *same* optimum level as we might during normal times. A sense of perspective can be helpful here so we can prioritize those tasks, processes, or goals that are most important. If we can willingly drop things that might be generally beneficial to the organization's success but aren't mission-critical right now, it will go a long way toward finding the bandwidth we need to continue during difficult circumstances.

This means we must stay dedicated to the practices that help us to be at our best physically, emotionally, and spiritually. This focus on self-care is often the first thing to go, but it is no frivolous matter, as we have seen. It is necessary to keep you at your most effective for decision-making and guidance.

Assuming we have done what we can to maintain a foundation of self-care and balance, we then move to decision-making. It can be tempting to respond to an urgent situation in kind, with fast decisions and quick about-faces. But this approach lacks any consideration for the inevitable change in circumstances that will occur (evolution of the situation) and leaves no room for innovation during the crisis. It can also lead to unintended miscommunication and give the appearance that the direction is not thoughtful or clear as you respond to unfolding circumstances. This can undermine a sense of confidence in the leadership and create a downward spiral of uncertainty within the entire organization.

Our role as leaders is to continue to lead from a place of inspiration and motivation and to be as transparent as possible along the way. Keeping the decision-making to a day-by-day or week-by-week process—rather than long-term prognostication—allows for a more fluid and dynamic response strategy in line with changing circumstances and creates an opportunity for more accurate communication to those you are serving. Everyone wants to think about the "what if" scenarios and immediately look out into the next few months or years, but this is not productive in a situation like a global pandemic in which everything is changing rapidly. It is best to plan and strategize in short bursts that align with the reality of what is unfolding in the present.

It is also important in crises or difficult situations for the leadership to remain positive. This doesn't mean putting on a big smiling face no matter the circumstances, but instead sharing the hope that your organization and your community will make it through whatever challenge is at hand. Staying positive is about faith in the future, not about disregarding the pain or suffering of the current moment.

For example, here is how we handled our Covid-19 response with a few of our key stakeholder groups during the pandemic:

AS LEADERS, OUR ROLE IS TO CONTINUE TO LEAD FROM A PLACE OF INSPIRATION AND MOTIVATION AND TO BE AS TRANSPARENT AS POSSIBLE ALL ALONG THE WAY.

- **Constituents:** Those we serve, like many in the world, were scared, in shock, and looking for ways to cope with their fears. We stopped most promotional activities and focused every channel we had (web, social media, magazines, booklets) on tools and resources for how to manage fear, cultivate health and well-being, find comfort and peace, and navigate the uncertainties of this time.
- **Donors:** As a nonprofit organization, we have a healthy fundraising program. We stopped all fundraising for eight months and simply reached out with phone calls, video calls, and letters to check on our donors and to offer tools of support, words of encouragement, and lots of prayer.
- **Associates:** With most of our associates headquartered on our campus at Unity Village, we sent everyone we could to the safety and comfort of their homes and did our best to equip them to work remotely as quickly as we could. We overcommunicated everything we did and took every precaution imaginable to ensure the safety of essential workers who needed to stay on campus. In addition, we made sure that no one lost their jobs during the pandemic and that all our business decisions were made with a primary focus on ensuring the health and safety of

all associates as we continued to serve our constituents.

The strategy worked and each stakeholder group responded positively to our approach. We did two things that were important along the way. Taking from the IT systems planning playbook and relying on what's called the agile method, we planned ahead in short bursts along each stage of the pandemic. We would imagine every possible scenario in terms of changes that could come as the pandemic evolved, considering the guidance from our local and regional government, and we planned what our response would be. As each new wave of restrictions or reopening occurred, we had a script for how to handle it. This allowed us to be responsive in real time to the changes. The second thing we did was prioritize people. Thinking of our associates, constituents, and donors, we placed ourselves in their shoes throughout and responded more as human beings having a dreadful shared experience than as corporate citizens focused on the bottom line.

The most valuable thing we learned through the process is that, though taxing and difficult, it is important to take each moment and each day as it is and only make decisions for that particular stage in the reality unfolding before us. For example, in the initial surges of the pandemic, our entire executive team met first thing every morning for a huddle to discuss what had changed in the past 24 hours and what adjustments needed to be made in response. Once those decisions were made, we could then communicate the information to all of our relevant stakeholder groups. This required significant effort, patience, and a lot of time, but transparent communications about what we did know, what we didn't know, and what actions we were taking provided a high level of comfort and confidence to our associates, donors, and constituents.

Some of the decisions we made during the pandemic were scary at first. The decision to stop promotions and focus on spiritual inspiration raised some eyebrows around our leadership table, but it paid off in the end. We had a record year in social media engagement and website traffic. Those products we stopped promoting—well, they experienced growth in almost every measurable category. We were reminded of a saying we had all heard at one time or another in our experience in Unity. "If you do the work (the work of Spirit), the rest will take care of itself." That certainly held true for us.

The only exception were the in-person events on our campus. Retreats, weddings, and corporate conferences came to a halt with the lockdown, just as our events, hotel, and food services had been gaining significant traction.

The decision to prioritize our associates' safety and ensure no job loss during this time resulted in tremendous positive feedback from our teams. They felt safe and cared for during a very difficult time. The leadership team received a steady stream of praise as people took the time to express their gratitude for our approach during such uncertain times, and productivity and commitment to our work were at all-time highs even as the associates learned to work from home.

Similarly, our decision to pause fundraising and simply check on the well-being of our major donors yielded positive results, although it took time. Donors felt appreciated and relationships were deepened as a result of our caring approach. As the pandemic waned briefly in early 2021, our annual giving trended up and we ended the fiscal year ahead of budget in most of our contribution categories.

When dealing with tough situations, leaders must acknowledge that the lines between the professional and the personal are bound to be blurred. This has never been more true than in our modern world, when technology makes it so easy for us to flip back and forth between work and home headspaces. Crises in the workplace can (and will) affect people on a personal level, and painful circumstances at home can (and will) affect people in their professional capacities. While there is no surefire way to address this dichotomy in all situations, having an awareness of this truth can prove invaluable when leading our organizations and caring for our communities. It's an important reminder to offer grace and compassion for whatever someone might be experiencing and to always return to our self-care practices, especially in difficult times.

STAYING
POSITIVE
IS ABOUT
FAITH IN THE
FUTURE, NOT
DISREGARDING
THE PAIN OR
SUFFERING OF
THE CURRENT
MOMENT.

A common mistake in response to crisis is to take no action at all. Many organizations struggle with analysis paralysis or find themselves simply waiting for clarity from another source. The clarity we hope for rarely emerges in a timely manner, and stakeholders are left wondering what is happening. It's always best to take some action toward planning and execution and to communicate it clearly, executing a response, even if you must change course later. Inaction and lack of communication with stakeholders will always lead to an outcome that is less than ideal and to a lack of confidence in leadership that isn't always easily repaired.

I have found that the best model to start with is to identify how the situation at hand affects each of your stakeholders. For instance, what is the impact to our associates, our customers, our shareholders or donors, our suppliers? If we carefully identify the potential impact to each party that is likely to be affected, we can then thoughtfully craft our next steps to best support each of them. Every action taken should be in support of their needs.

This practice ensures that we consider the unique circumstances for each stakeholder and that we're applying our best efforts to support them. Each stakeholder group will have their own specific needs, but they will all need to feel seen and heard and to know that you understand what they're dealing with. And don't be afraid to overcommunicate. The more information and transparency you can provide, the more confident and supported your stakeholders will feel. When someone is facing difficult circumstances, hearing nothing at all is almost always worse than hearing there is no concrete plan yet.

Every crisis is different and will call for different strategies. Regardless of the circumstances, however, taking each unique stakeholder into account, striving to support their needs and to communicate early, often, and thoroughly, and making decisions only as far as you can see will help you succeed in navigating the situation.

Failing Can Be Your Friend Too

When it comes to crisis situations, most understand and accept that there is nothing we can do to steer clear of all of them. But when it comes to failure, many take their fear to a dangerous level of avoidance. We live in a culture that has long been conditioned to see failure as something bad, to be avoided at almost any cost. While we know logically that we're bound to face hiccups, obstacles, setbacks, and even tragedies, this knowledge can be harmful. We can get lost in worrying about potential scenarios and what might happen in the long term. As we contemplate making a change or making a decision, we get stalled by analysis paralysis. The "what if" questions can prove overwhelming.

Do not be discouraged. Return to your meditation practice and be present with what you can control today, in this moment, instead of considering what the situation might be a year from now, a month from now, or even tomorrow. You're not there right now, so you can't control those hypotheticals. Worry today cannot ensure your success later. Make a positive difference with what is in front of you and allow the rest to unfold.

As much as we may want business to be straightforward, mistake-free, and easy to predict, that's just not how it works. Thankfully, in the early 2000s, a significant movement started—largely in Silicon Valley—built on the premise that if you are not failing in some efforts, you are not innovating enough. Just as intuition is becoming an important strength in corporate environments, the value of failure has been transformed. In fact, the idea of failure has made an about-face, from something that should be prevented whenever possible to something that's not only acceptable but can be a positive experience. Slogans and memes have emerged, encouraging people to "fail forward" or "fail fast" and "fail often." Best-selling books have been written on how best to fail (and recover) in various aspects of business operations.

It was from this new perspective that I found a connection to spiritual principles. This new fail-forward movement is based on the simple idea that it is okay to fail. Failure is not the end; it's an opportunity to learn what you can from the experience and apply it to the next iteration. The act of failing no longer spells doom for your entire company or even that specific endeavor—it's just a blip on the journey to growth, as long as you are able to learn from the experience and apply that new knowledge to your continued evolution. We can understand failure as an occurrence, not as a reflection of ourselves. Experiencing failure does not make *you* a failure.

What happens when we look at this concept through a spiritual lens? Charles Fillmore, cofounder of Unity, defines failure as an "inability through a lack of power to make a demonstration. Seeming failure is often a stepping-stone to something higher." We also find an important reference in scripture to failure: "You know if a man falls down, he gets up again. And if a man goes the wrong way, he turns around and comes back" (Jeremiah 8:4). In both references, we find that failure is not the end. Failure does not define a person or an organization. Instead, we find guidance for learning from the missteps we've taken and encouragement to continue the journey with new knowledge.

The most innovative and successful people and organizations have experienced failure on occasion. It's just one stage of the journey toward your vision. If we're able to minimize our focus on the failure, we can maximize our focus on how to best move forward. Failures can act as a compass to aid our navigation.

Too many times, we see failure not as a compass but as a hammer, and we use that hammer to beat ourselves up or demolish our progress. We fail once and walk away, not realizing that the next effort—with applied modification—would allow us to reach our desired outcome.

One of my own experiences with failure involved a significant software project for Unity. The platform that was essential to running our nonprofit was more than 10 years old. It was specifically designed to support our publishing operations, which it did very well, but a big part of a nonprofit's operations is also donor and constituent stewardship. These days there are powerful platforms to help build rich and meaningful relationships with your constituents, allowing you to create customized content that serves them specifically. Though we had customized our own publishing platform to do some of this, we were missing the most powerful pieces of this component.

After several months of research, we chose what we thought was a good fit to help us better serve our constituents and deepen our relationships with our donors with the potential to transform our service. But after nine months of work, we realized the publishing operations provided by the new platform were not robust enough to handle our many magazine publications and complex promotions and acquisitions. We paused the project and candidly rehashed what was going well and what wasn't, and we were frank with one another about

FAILURE IS NOT THE END; IT'S AN OPPORTUNITY TO LEARN WHAT YOU CAN FROM THE EXPERIENCE AND APPLY IT TO THE NEXT ITERATION.

the delays and disappointments. Despite our wealth of IT experience and leadership, we found ourselves in that age-old trap where a project costs more and takes longer than we ever imagined and losing some of our existing capabilities in the quest to improve others.

Our vendor brought a new partner to the table—a partner who had written some add-on pieces of software they thought would fit the bill for our needs. Despite our frustration, we decided to remain positive and vigilant, and we restarted the project with the new partner on board. Six months later we found ourselves in the same place. The new add-on code was still not what we needed.

At this point, we were more than a year and a half into the project, with tens of thousands of dollars spent, and no foreseeable product or real potential for a date to go live with the new platform. At this point, our conclusion was that it would cost significantly more in time and money to continue than it would to scrap the effort and begin again. We terminated the project.

In many of the organizations I've served previously, this would have been a huge drama leading to termination notices or hurting the reputations of the project's leaders. Both the project and its champions would be regarded as failures. But because we had established a culture of innovation, from the board to each of our associates, this was not the case.

Sure, people were frustrated and disappointed—no one was excited that this process was taking so long without the result we wanted to see—but instead of pointing fingers and getting caught up in the blame game, the focus very quickly shifted to identifying what we had learned from the experience and how we could use those lessons to move forward. Our strategic vision remained the primary goal, even when things weren't going to plan. Board members actually congratulated us for facing facts and making the tough decision. We restarted the project with a greater understanding of our own complex operations and a clearer vision of our needs.

Whenever a decision or change ends in failure, it's important to remember that we are never "less than" because we have failed at something. We cannot allow mistakes and missteps to define us. Our unchanging identity is that of a powerful and unique strand of the Divine expressing here on earth. As such we can lean into that concept and remind ourselves that we are not our outer appearance, the choices we have made, or the failures we have experienced. The truth of who we are remains the sentient intelligence that lies back of all of that. If we can remind ourselves of that, we can maintain our self-worth despite the outer circumstance.

Failure is temporary, and sometimes it is simply part of the process. It doesn't last forever, and it can even offer us plenty to learn along the way. Other times, failure is a sign that it's time to walk away or reverse course. It may show us a dead end or a limit we didn't know was there. How are we to know the difference?

We must return to our intuition, to the wisdom that lies within our own heart. Be still, listen, and you will know. It can be hard to do, especially if you haven't practiced that stillness—or if you just don't like the answer you get. But as you practice how to listen to your intuition, trust your gut, and act in alignment with your heart, this will get easier and easier.

Gems from Part Four: Handling Change, Crisis, and Failure

- Make change your friend! This is the simplest and most impactful way for you to adjust your thinking. Change is inevitable—it's universal law.

- Recognize your own resistance to whatever has occurred. Resistance is indeed futile and causes unnecessary pain. But you can choose what happens next.

- Acceptance doesn't make you a doormat; it means focusing on solutions. Instead of lamenting *what is* or hiding your head in the sand, take positive action steps.

- When you respond from a center of peace, you can be far more productive than you ever thought.

- When forced to focus on what could go wrong (contingency plans), balance it by imagining the best possible outcomes too.

- The key to managing a crisis? Stay committed to your spiritual practice and self-care.
- When faced with a personal loss or tragedy, make room to feel the grief and anguish. Be present to the pain and experience it fully and out loud.
- Seek professional counseling, a neutral party to help explore your thoughts and feelings and develop a sense of peace. Find small getaways—movies, books, prayer, exercise—for your mental and emotional well-being.
- When leading others through a crisis, focus on what is mission critical and postpone other good ideas for a better time.
- Take your time making decisions. Miscommunication and abrupt changes in direction do not inspire confidence in those you are leading.
- A crisis is a crucial time to be transparent. Keep everyone up to date on the latest developments, even if you have to say "I don't know yet" about future possibilities.
- Offer grace and compassion for what others are experiencing. Be mindful of how the situation affects each group of stakeholders—associates, customers, shareholders, donors, suppliers. Each will have specific needs you can support.

- Don't let fear of failure make you miserable worrying about the future or keep you from trying new things. Failure is an opportunity to learn and do better next time. Experiencing failure does not make *you* a failure.

- Sometimes failure is part of the process and sometimes it's a sign to walk away. Your intuition will tell you the difference if you have developed it with a stillness practice.

Epilogue

Moving Forward

As leaders in this modern world, we are asked to balance all manner of priorities day in and day out. As more demands are placed on our time and attention than ever before, it may seem counterintuitive to return to ancient teachings rather than merely looking for a cutting-edge solution to our challenges. But what we learn when we look to the spiritual guidance of the ages is that these principles and practices have withstood the tests of time for good reason.

Instead of simply striving to find balance between projects and initiatives or between success at work and peace at home, seeking an internal equilibrium makes it possible to show up as our very best in any situation—and to accept whatever the outcome might be so we can keep moving forward, keep showing up as our most optimal and most authentic selves.

When we learn to trust our intuition, value our own health and wellness, and promote a sense of purpose among the organizations we lead, we create an opportunity to achieve both greater success and increased well-being. Like the pebble in a pond, this creates a ripple effect of positivity throughout our lives and our communities. And isn't that what we're all hoping to do?

Acknowledgments

I want to thank the Unity World Headquarters Board of Directors for believing in me and taking a chance on me as a first-time CEO.

I would like to thank the Unity executive team for its partnership, patience, and wisdom as we cocreated a compassionate, innovative culture and a path toward organizational transformation and success.

A warm thank-you to every Unity associate for your support, transparency, commitment, and the awesome opportunity to serve alongside you. Much of the learning in this book and the resulting successes are because of the amazing individuals I have served with and learned from during my tenure. They are equally as responsible for the good works that have been accomplished. I bow to each of you in gratitude.

A special thanks to the many spiritual mentors and teachers who have contributed to my spiritual growth, maturity, and self-realization. My life would not be as rich without your guidance, wisdom, and support throughout my journey.

I would also like to thank all those through the years who helped me develop my skills and grow my experience. Gratitude to all of my former leaders, colleagues, teammates, partners, and even the companies that provided some of the difficult environments that brought about these insights.

And finally, heartfelt acknowledgment to my wife and daughter who have always seen in me more than I have been able to see in myself and for always lifting me up. We are a small tribe but a mighty one.